taste

derbyshire Issue 3

Welcome to the third edition of taste derbyshire, a book packed with exciting new, tried and tasted recipes.

The taste derbyshire kitchen was a hive of activity from January to April and it was a delight to have the fridges and pantry stocked to overflowing with such a selection of beautiful produce.

James, Jane, Charlotte and Victoria are the main cooks in this edition, each bringing their own unique talents and specialities literally to the table, and they have created some great culinary delights for you to try. Our aim is to produce good food for people with busy lifestyles, as well as one or two recipes which take just a little bit longer to create.

Jeanette, once again, has provided some stunning photography under stressful conditions, which we hope will give you inspiration for presentation.

We are also delighted to feature Rachael Green. This year she has provided us with three mouthwatering recipes. We would also like to thank the professional chefs who have contributed their own favourites, which we believe, add an extra special dimension to taste derbyshire

Please enjoy our third edition

Jane Plant

Editor

Sales Executives
James John Cave
Scott David Burgess
Carol Ann Wilson
Lisa Ava O'Reilly
Victoria Isabella Plant

The Cooking Team
James John Cave
Jane Elizabeth Plant
Charlotte Elizabeth Burgess
Victoria Isabella Plant

Sleeping Partner
Indiana Eve Burgess

Photography.
Jeanette Marie Howe
at Jen Photography 07793 739684
www.gravityrides.co.uk

Design
David Robert Dykes
at Copper Dog Ltd
Luke Mellor

Printed by Buxton Press

IMAGES
PUBLISHING

LIMITED

Victoria House,
Market Place, Crich. DE4 5DD

01773 850050
www.tastederbyshire.co.uk

inside taste derbyshire

we meet the 'food' people of Derbyshire who make it happen. Here are just a few.

100 pages of recipes

Don't miss…
pages 142 to 179. There you can find the people that can help you create the dishes in taste derbyshire

Derbyshire **producers** unearthed

A taste of
Derbyshire
honey

The Honey Pot

Here in the county of Derbyshire we are blessed with a diverse area that makes our honey amongst the finest in the world. Our parks and gardens, towns and villages, the Derbyshire Dales and the Peak District produce the best local honey.

With beekeepers who care for their bees and show a passion in the craft, this has helped to separate quality products from the imported honeys sold by the majority of the shops.

The Honey Pot based at Markeaton Park Craft Village, Derby, has been trading since 1990 and provides the best Derbyshire honey from their own private apiaries, caring for about fifty beehives in the best of locations. The Honey Pot also supplies the Derbyshire beekeepers with their equipment to help them to keep up with the demand for their honey.

Their customers are fascinated by the range of goods that are associated with the craft of beekeeping, as well as their Derbyshire clear and set honey, they also have heather honey from the Peak

District and comb honey including chunk honey. But that's not all, there are health products, beeswax candles and polishes, honey dippers, beekeeping equipment as well as a few gifts for the children to try.

For the second year running, The Honey Pot has won the Challenge Cup for getting the most points at the Derbyshire Beekeepers Association honey show, held each year at Carsington Water Visitors Centre, including the cup for the best Derbyshire Heather Honey and the Composite Cup for the best of three different honeys.

The Honey Pot has been doing the monthly Farmers' Markets at Belper and Bakewell for several years as well as the Bakewell Show in the Food and Farming marquee.

Finding a good supply is not always easy to source, but with the help of taste derbyshire you can support your local beekeeper and buy Derbyshire honey from The Honey Pot.

The Honey Pot, Markeaton Park Craft Village, Markeaton Lane, Derby, DE22 3BG.
Tel: 01332 203893 www.localhoney.co.uk

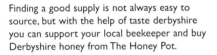

Award winning
Lemon Oil

Olive oil and Vinegars are a common sight on the shelves of supermarkets and delicatessens up and down the country, but it is unlikely you will find some of the flavours that Steve Croot of Field House Foods has come up with. Steve, who is a well known herb grower from Duffield, Derbyshire gives us some tips on using olive oil and some information about the range of oils and vinegars his company produces and how to use them.

Cooking with Olive Oil

Olive oils differ in quality, smokepoint, colour, flavour and aroma. Each type of olive oil has its own purpose. Extra virgin oil has the richest, deepest flavour and captures the essence of the olive itself, but isn't appropriate for every dish. Cooking reduces the flavour of extra-virgin oil. Save it for salads and other cold dishes. Pure olive oil is used as a base oil by Field House Foods as it has a relatively high smoke point and therefore makes it good as a cooking oil.

Healthier Eating

There's now a wealth of evidence to suggest that olive oil has many health benefits. That's because olive oil is rich in monounsaturates, and these help to reduce the risk of heart disease, by lowering the LDL or "bad cholesterol" and increasing the HDL or "good cholesterol". Olive oil is also a great source of vitamin A and E, both of which help to protect cells and tissue. Some researchers believe that monounsaturates can help the skin to resist the activity of damaging free radicals and that these fats are also associated with less wrinkling.

Health guidelines say that no more than one-third of our daily calorie intake should come from fat, with around 12 per cent of the total coming from monounsaturates.

Here are a few ways in which you could add more olive oil to your diet...

• Use olive oil when you roast potatoes or vegetables.
• Add a drizzle of olive oil to your mashed potatoes, instead of butter.
• Lightly drizzled olive oil makes a great substitute for butter or margarine in sandwiches.
• Instead of butter or lard, make delicious fried eggs or succulent sausages by cooking in a little olive oil.

Field House Foods produce a range of flavoured oils, a number of which have won Great Taste Awards. All these oils can be used for cooking or with salads and other cold dishes. Steve Croot is particularly proud of the company's award winning lemon oil. "We sell so much of it at farmers markets and food fairs, it is fantastic for pan frying fish or chicken but can also be used as a dressing on its own, or mixed with a vinegar as a dressing"

The company produces a fantastic range of oils including, lemon, garlic, lime, chilli, basil, rosemary, sun-dried tomato, mandarin, orange and lemongrass. So why not give them a try, there is a flavour to suit everyone in their collection.

Field House Foods also stock a range of vinegars to complement the oils – including their best selling product Balsamic Vinegar with Basil.

Steve Croot

www.fieldhousefoods.com   Tel: 0141 416 1411

STANDARDS
of
EXCELLENCE

Do you know that
Chesterfield boasts a
specialist tea and coffee
business that has been
established for over
48 years?

Northern Tea Merchants has a very interesting history. In 1926, Albert Pogson, having moved to Chesterfield from Lincoln took a sales position that was offered by 'The Ceylon Tea Growers Association' (based in Nottingham) to develop the Chesterfield area for them and increase their door-to-door sales business. He undertook this task with a will and soon was promoted to the position of Van Sales Superintendent. (The vans in question were Model 'T' Fords!) In 1936, he decided that he could do the job better for himself. He established the 'Spire Tea Company' and commenced selling tea door to door under his own name, wearing plus fours, a bowler hat and driving an Austin 7 Van. The unfortunate onset of World War in 1939 meant that tea was rationed, which made trading very difficult. Despite this, his business continued to flourish, and when tea ceased to be rationed in the mid-1950s he was still trading and had cultivated many loyal customers, some of whom are still purchasing tea from the Pogson family today, some 60 years later!

His son, David was born in 1937, and inherited his father's passion for tea. He says…"One of my earliest memories was the delightful smell that filled my father's office and the fascinating markings from far-away places that were stencilled on the tea chests in his store-room."

Having left school in 1953, David commenced work with his father until 1959, when the entrepreneurial spirit drove

him to establish his own tea company (in a different area to that which Albert had cultivated), and Northern Tea Merchants was born.

In the early 1960s, an invention that was to change the shape of tea drinking in the UK was launched - The tea bag. David realised how revolutionary this idea was and by 1965 was selling his own. He then purchased a tea bag machine that would make 250 tea bags per minute and things started to take off. By this time he was employing 5 members of staff and using 2 vans to deliver his goods to both retail and wholesale customers. In 1971, Albert (aged 70), retired and his business was amalgamated with Northern Tea Merchants customer base.

From these beginnings, David has taken every opportunity to expand his business and widen his interest in the world's

teas and coffees. He now employs 25 members of staff, and owns 5 vans, which are in daily use delivering within a radius of 150 miles from Chesterfield. Northern Tea Merchants are specialist contract packers of Organic Teas, Coffees and Cocoa, they support ardently the FairTrade concept, and offer their specialist services to any company who wish to improve the quality of their teas and coffees.

The Tea Council is the mouthpiece of the UK Tea Trade and devote their time and (considerable) budget to improving the British public's perception of tea. To this end, they created a 'Guild', which would promote standards of excellence in the presentation and service of tea to the public. Only establishments that are of a high quality are invited to join. Naturally, Northern Tea Merchants was a member from early in the Guild's history. It is the desire to pass on his passion for tea that has driven David to extensively refurbish his shop on Chatsworth Road, Chesterfield, with the introduction of a range of light meals and tasty lunches to complement the vast range of excellent quality teas and coffees already sold. There is even a set of pairings of tea and food offered that have been devised by the Tea Council and the Academy Of Food And Wine where the tea complements the food served! Northern Tea Merchant's menu of beverages spans over 60 pages and is also an insight into the history of tea, its countries of origin, its flavour and the best way to brew the marvellous leaf.

The first thing that you experience when you enter this emporium of taste is the heady aroma of tea and coffee. Then, whilst your olfactory nerves are still reeling from the delicious smells, your eyes take in the beautifully lit, classically presented layout of the shop. The shelves on the left-hand side offer teas from all over the world, beautifully packed in the distinctive gold packaging that Northern Tea Merchants use. There is, to the centre of the shop, a series of large bins that contain some of the world's finest freshly roasted coffees, which can be purchased as beans, or ground for no extra charge. A series of wonderful circular tables graces the right hand side of the shop, whose glass tops cover samples of 36 different teas and coffees from the huge range supplied.

Whilst you sit with your chosen drink, your eyes wander around the walls which are covered with historic quotations about tea and coffee and fascinating insights into the way that tea and coffee has been marketed throughout the last century. David has also recently completed work on a special tasting room in which he can demonstate the science AND the magic that goes into creating Northern Tea Merchants' world renowned blends. There is talk of private tasting sessions and guided tours of the tea manufacturing room and coffee roastery in the near future. Please telephone 01246 232600 for details.

David's favourite quotation is the Chinese Poet Lu-Wah's 'Tea is water bewitched'. Tea has bewitched him since he was a child. Come and share his infectious enthusiasm. You will be bewitched too.

Brazil Santos
A good 'middle of the road' type with a smooth, mild flavour

Ching Wo Tea
Ideal for afternoon tea with its bright copper infusion, light flavour and aroma

Earl Grey Tea
Flavoured with oil of Bergamot it produces a delightful citrus flavour

Gunpowder Green Tea
The tightly rolled grey-green leaves unfurl when infused and have a slightly fruity flavour

The Original Farmers' Market Shop is a small, independent business and has been trading since 2001. They offer a range of high quality local and British produce. They still operate on the Farmers' Market rules, aiming to source as much as possible within a 30 mile radius of the shop.

Goods are sourced from further a-field if there are no suitable local producers. In these cases they choose selected items from independent British specialist food producers. Only items not grown in Britain, such as tea coffee, olives and some herbs and spices are sourced from abroad. They offer free range and organic options where possible. Central to their philosophy is knowing the source of their products - knowing the farmers and suppliers and working in partnership with them. They now specialise in healthier, Gluten Free products including pies, biscuits, burgers, cakes, flour, muesli, sausage and ready meals made from local produce.

THE ORIGINAL
FARMERS MARKET SHOP

Their product range has increased in the four years of trading. They now offer an outdoor catering service - and can prepare your special dinner party using all their quality products. They pride themselves in their online services, offering next day delivery and Saturday shipping services. Not to mention their in store collect service, allowing customers to reserve produce via the Internet then collect at a time and date suited to them from their Bakewell shop. As expected all shipping charges are refunded from the order.

They look forward to seeing you soon, either in person or if you can't call in, online. 01629 815814.

E-mail postmaster@thefarmersmarketshop.co.uk

Sparkling Wine at
'Chateau Renishaw'

The vineyards at Renishaw Hall in Derbyshire have been
producing a sparkling wine since 2002 when the quality of the
grape became good enough and it was decided at
Sir Reresby Sitwell's suggestion to try a sparkling wine. It is just
recently that the grape yield has been such that more bottles
can now be produced, making the wine available for sale.

The Renishaw Vineyards produce the Seyval Blanc grape, the new German Phoenix variety, and Madeleine Angevine and it is the Seyval Blanc grape that is separated at harvest and used to produce the sparkling wine.

The same initial process is used in the first year of production, as in the still wine, but instead of being bottled to drink at the end of this period, sugar is added and a 'crown' cap placed on the champagne bottle and it is left for another year. To become quality sparkling wine it needs to be left for a minimum of 9 months, Renishaw Sparkling Wine is left for 12 months before taste-testing for quality to ensure that it is ready for the final process. February saw the 2004 wine being taken to the Three Choirs Vineyard in Gloucestershire to complete this process and the sparkling wine went on sale in limited quantities at Renishaw Hall at Easter.

the
Perfect
Pint

In August 2006 The Kestrel, Marehay became the first freehouse in Amber Valley to be awarded The British Beer & Pub Association Gold Award for the quality of the beers, an award scheme which was introduced in 2006. At the time there were about 40 awards in the whole of the UK. At the time of writing this article the total had reached 100.

The Gold award, which covers cask, keg and bottled products, involves a two hour detailed survey of the beer cellar and bars by a Cask Marque Inspector, to check that standards of hygiene are high and the correct temperature is maintained.

Phil Barnaville, who has the primary function of looking after the beers, explains why his could be the perfect pint. Phil who is a postgraduate in biochemical sciences has a background in the science of brewing and brewing analysis and a passion for detail- scary!

As with all award processes the goal is achieved by hard work, attention to detail and regular testing, the latter bringing the greatest satisfaction.

The process of producing the perfect pint starts with the supplier. If they manage their part of the process by keeping the cask and keg beers at the correct storage temperature (55°F) and then deliver them to your cellar in good condition, you are halfway there.

The work in the cellar ensures that the beers are ready to be served in the right condition and at the right temperature and that the beer is served in clean beers lines. In the cellar this means clearing any spillages, washing surfaces and cleaning any equipment that is involved in the dispensing of Keg & cask Beers on a regular basis, and monitoring the equipment (especially the cellar cooling equipment) to ensure it is

operating properly. Establishing a good relationship with the brewery's technical services is essential in maintaining the equipment.

Central to the process of dispense are the beer lines. Over the years, the supplying brewery has changed these when they were suspected of not being up to the standard that Phil wants to maintain in providing beers in excellent condition. The problems with beer quality that are often encountered in some establishments are when, in the interests of economy, the beer lines are not cleaned regularly or with the correct solution. Having found a good supplier of the most suitable beer line cleaner, the lines at The Kestrel are cleaned every week. This may cost up to 70 pints per week (there are two

Philip Barnaville, BA, MSC.

Venting the barrel

Checking clarity

bars) but Phil believes it is worth it. He's a bit of a fanatic. How many times have you had a bad pint and not returned to the pub.

Then we come to the serving. You may have the best range of beers but if they are served in a poorly presented glass then the beer will lose its sparkle. It is often argued that rinse aide in mechanical glass washers leaves behind a film in the glass and the first pint removes it. Then you re-use the glass. Notwithstanding the hygiene issues of cross contamination, a fresh glass is always used at The Kestrel. However, the use of a glass cleaner under the brand name of "Renovate" is used on a regular basis to remove the rinse aid and, as important, the glass washer is cleaned after each use.

Each night the taps are removed from the beer fonts and washed with water then placed in soda water. The cask delivery pipes are also washed with soda water to remove any beer residues.

Too much detail? Possibly, but the work by Phil, Martin and Sarah in maintaining high standards in all aspects of the business has allowed them to grow and expand their business.

The Kestrel Inn at Marehay
51 Upper Marehay Road
Ripley Derbyshire DE5 8JF

01773 743970

Award winning cellar

The Kestrel Inn

The Q Butchers Guide To Cooking Meat

How do we guarantee that the beef, pork or lamb
that we cook will turn out okay?
The Guild of Q Butchers provides some interesting guidelines into
cooking Sunday lunch or an informal al fresco barbeque.
Here are the basic cooking times and tips
for beef, lamb, and pork.

COOKING TIPS FOR BEEF AND LAMB
(credits to EBLEX - www.beefyandlamby.co.uk)
There are many delicious ways to cook Quality Standard
beef and lamb.
This section gives you great tips on how to cook beef and
lamb successfully, whichever way you choose to cook it.

Meat storage and preparation

Ensure that hands, equipment and surfaces are scrupulously
clean before and after handling food and between handling
raw and cooked foods - especially when using the barbeque.
Check your fridge is operating at the correct temperature:
between 0 and 4 degrees centigrade.
Keep a separate hard, durable chopping board for preparing
raw meats.
Defrost frozen foods thoroughly (unless otherwise stated)
and do not re-freeze once thawed.
Cover and store raw and cooked foods separately. Store
uncooked foods lower in the refrigerator than cooked ones.
Make sure foods are thoroughly and evenly defrosted, and
when re-heating ensure piping hot throughout.
When marinating meat, cover and store in a refrigerator.
Ensure burgers and sausages are thoroughly cooked and
piping hot before serving.
When roasting a stuffed joint remember to weigh the joint
after stuffing, then calculate the cooking time.
Food thermometers can be used to ensure internal food
temperatures are sufficiently hot.

Stir-frying

Stir-frying is an ideal quick method of cooking meat as the
thin strips cook in only a few minutes.
It is only necessary to use a very small amount of oil (1
tablespoon) when stir-frying. Use a vegetable based oil which
can be heated to higher temperatures.
Use a non-stick wok or large frying pan. Always ensure that
the pan or wok is really hot before adding the meat a little
at a time - it should sizzle when the pieces are added.
The meat should ideally be trimmed of excess fat and cut

into approximately 1cm (½") strips, cut across the grain to
help tenderise the meat and prevent shrinkage.

Method

Heat 15ml (1tbsp) oil in a wok or large frying pan.
Add the meat and stir-fry for the recommended time.
Add the hardest vegetables first (e.g carrots, onions) and
cook for 2-3 minutes before adding the rest.
Add sauce (up to 150ml(1/4pt)) and cook for a further
couple of minutes.

Guide to roasting

Roasting doesn't need to be complicated. Simply weigh the
raw joint and calculate the cooking time using the table
below to ensure the meat is cooked to your liking.

Roasting essentials

Position the oven shelves so that the meat is in the centre
of the oven.
Place the joint uncovered on a wire rack in a roasting tin
ensuring any fat is on the top. This allows the juices to run
down and baste the joint naturally.
When roasting beef and lamb joints, cook them in a
moderate oven for slightly longer to ensure even cooking.
Remember to weigh beef and lamb joints before calculating
your preferred cooking time.
Allow the joint to rest for 5-10 minutes after cooking to let
the meat fibres relax and juices distribute evenly so the joint
is moist and easy to carve.
The degree of cooking can be tested easily using a meat
thermometer towards the end of the cooking time: insert
into the centre of the joint or at the thickest point, until it
reaches the required temperature.
Beef: Rare - 60°C, Medium - 70°C, Well Done - 80°C
Lamb: Medium - 70-75°C, Well Done - 75-80°C

Roasting in liquid

Slow moist methods include pot roasting, stewing, braising
and casseroling. These methods are ideal for tenderising less
expensive, less tender cuts of meat and are convenient ways

joints are ideal for pot roasting.

It is traditionally carried out by browning the joint and then cooking in the oven or on the hob with liquid and vegetables.

Allow approximately 450g (1lb) vegetables (use root vegetables cut into large pieces) and 150ml (¼pt) liquid (try stock, wine, cider, beer etc) for a 1.25kg (2½lb) joint.

Method

Heat 15ml(1tbsp) oil in a large heavy based saucepan or casserole dish. Brown the joint on all sides.

Add the vegetables and liquid, and any seasoning or herbs. Cover and cook either on the hob on a low simmer or in the oven for the calculated cooking time.

Stewing, braising and casseroling

Stews and casseroles use cubed meat, while braising traditionally uses whole steaks or chops.

As with pot roasting the meat is simmered at a low temperature on the hob or in the oven with added liquid.

Allow approximately 225-350g (8-12oz) vegetables (use root vegetables cut into chunks) per 450g (1lb) meat and 150ml (1/4pt) liquid (try stock, wine, beer etc).

Method

It is not necessary to pre-seal the meat first, just add all the ingredients to a large pan or casserole dish, cover and cook for recommended time.

You could also try adding jars of shop bought sauces to make preparation really quick. This method is ideal for making tasty curries, simply add a jar of shop-bought curry sauce to some cubed meat and vegetables and cook for the calculated cooking time.

Barbeque tips

Light barbeques well in advance, making sure you use enough charcoal, and wait until it is glowing red (with a powdery grey surface) before starting to cook.

Keep meat refrigerated for as long as possible before cooking.

Make sure the chef doesn't mix up the cooking utensils, boards or plates for raw and cooked meats - keep them separate.

Always wash hands thoroughly - before preparing food, after touching raw meat and before eating.

Ensure all sausages and burgers are thoroughly cooked before serving (juices should run clear).

of cooking as they require very little preparation or attention during cooking. Simply pop one in the oven or on the hob and let it cook while you sit and relax.

As it is all cooked in one pot you'll save on washing up too!!

Pot roasting

Pot roasting uses whole joints of meat - boned and rolled

Pan-frying

Pan-frying, or 'shallow frying' is a quick cooking method for

small, tender cuts using an uncovered pan on the hob.
Use a heavy-based frying pan, sauté pan or wok.
For best results, use only a small quantity of oil or butter.
Ensure that the oil is hot before adding your preferred beef
or lamb cuts.
Sear each side quickly to seal in juices and retain succulence.
Only turn your steaks once during cooking; leaving them to
cook untouched will produce juicier results.

Grilling

A fast, dry alternative to pan-frying for cooking tender cuts,
using intense radiant heat either above or below the meat.
Char-grilling or barbequing, seals the meat juices by forming
a crust on the surface of the meat. The meat must be basted
with a prepared glaze, butter, oil or reserved marinade
mixture. This gives a distinctive flavour to your beef or lamb
and keeps the meat moist and succulent. Only turn your
steaks once during cooking; leaving them to cook untouched
will produce juicier results.

Under The Heat.

Cook the food under a heated element such as a
conventional electric or gas grill.

Over The Heat.

Brush the meat lightly with oil and ensure that the grill rack
is pre-heated. Place the grill rack over a gas or charcoal grill
or barbeque.

Between Heat.

Place the meat between heated grill bars (such as vertical
toaster or grill.) This employs radiant heat, convection heat
or both.

Baking

This method employs dry cooking in the oven – either in a
roasting tin or in a sealed container or foil 'packet'. For
wonderfully tender meat, choose a clay or terracotta 'brick'
which effectively creates a clay oven within your oven. As
the oven heats, steam condenses in the pot, basting the meat
in its own juices. The end result is moist, tender, full of
flavour and naturally cooked with no extra fat.

Colin Wright from Wrights Butchers, Codnor is a member of Guild of Q Butchers

Staff of Andrew Armstrongs Butchers Shop Bakewell, Armstrong Butchers are members of the Guild of Q Butchers.

Mainstream Meats
the areas leading catering butcher

Mainstream Meats pride themselves on being the areas leading catering butcher. Meat is sourced direct from local farms, transported to the local abattoir and then delivered to their premises to reduce the food miles and ensure the animals welfare.

They offer a butchering service to local farmers for them to supply to the public, many of their farmer customers are now opening farm shops due to their success, they are also their suppliers of pork, beef & lamb. The farmers allow us to visit their farms to select the cattle and observe the animals welfare.

Mainstream hang their beef for 21-28 days to ensure quality, flavour and tenderness. The most common remark they hear is "It's like beef used to taste".

The list of farmers they deal with is quite impressive:

Richard & Clare Aldis of Hardwick Park Farm, Hardwick Hall, Richard & Clare's farm shop opened 17.03.07.

Neil & Jill Haslam of Broad Nook Farm, Neil & Jill are currently converting an out building into a farm shop.

Dave & Sarah Hunt of Manor Farm Fold, Oakerthorpe, Dave & Sarah breed Highland cattle producing traditional beef which is in such high demand they have more customers than meat.

Danny & Charlotte Lowe of Unthank Hall Farm, Holmesfield, Danny & Charlotte produce quality pork & beef on their farm that has been in the family for over 400 years sell their produce on Farmers Markets.

Robert & Helen Helliwell of Upper Booth Farm, Edale, Robert & Helen produce quality beef from their herd of belted Galloway's.

Brenda Harrop of New Farm, Alport Youlgreave, breeder of rare breed pork such as Saddleback pigs & Gloucester Old Spots, Brenda is highly regarded for the cattle she produces.

William & Janet Biggin of Cordwell Farm Holmesfield, supplier of Derbyshire Turkey.

Mainstream Meats also produce a quality sausage, winning four awards at last year's meatex. Their butchers are trained butchers are trained to NVQ level, and they insist on quality breeds such as Aberdeen Angus & Hereford.

Neil and Jill Haslam
Broad Nook Farm, Nottingham Road
Selston
Phone: 01773 812015

Dear Paul,
Neil and I would like to thank you and your team of butchers for providing an outstanding service for our home produced beef. Over the last 18 months we have learned from you and value your many years of experience.

The cuts of meat and steak are all prepared to an excellent standard and packed and labelled clearly. Our customers are really happy and surprised at the quality and presentation of the beef.

We also appreciate the help and advice you have given us and your willingness to suggest ways to progress our business further.

It is a pleasure dealing with you and we hope to continue our relationship for many years to come.

Thank you for your patience and understanding.

Yours sincerely
Jill Haslam. Broad Nook Farm

Hardwick Park Farm
Norwood Lane, Norwood
February 2007

Mainstream International Foods Limited have been our butchers for the past 18 months after being recommended to us by another butcher. Our meat retail sales knowledge was limited in the beginning, but with the help and support of a dedicated team at Mainstream this has gone from strength to strength over the past 18 months. They have helped us maximise our meat potential with not only their vast knowledge of what the consumer wants, but also with how to maximise the profitability of each of our animals.

Mainstream butcher lambs, pigs & cattle for us on a weekly basis for us, not only offering us a fantastic butchery service, but also a vast array of ideas for delicious burgers and sausages. They have helped us set up and secure local business contracts and they have played a major part in the selling of our own meat direct to the general public. So much so that they have encouraged us 100% in the setting up of our own farm shop and shared with us in our success.

Mainstreams vast catering and retail butchery knowledge and experience is self evident in the produce that they return to us. Our meat is always beautifully butchered, presented, packaged and labelled, and any special requests that our customers make are never too much trouble for them.

Mainstream International Foods Ltd are an extremely professional and well managed company, and we would have no hesitation in recommending their Services to any new customers.

Clare & Richard Aldis.
R & C Aldis Farming Ltd

12 December 2006
Dear Paul

It's been about a year now since our association with you began and we are so pleased with the way things are going, we just had to put pen to paper.

Since you have been butchering our beef, our sales have almost trebled. The presentation and traceability of the meat makes all the difference. The steaks and joints are cut perfectly into meal-sized portions and the packing and labelling give it all the professional touch. Your obliging, helpful and "can do" attitude is much appreciated and we can always rely on you to make sure our beef is hung for the perfect amount of time.

Once the animal has left our hands it's nice to be able to relax and be confident that you and the guys at Mainstream will take care of all the rest. When we first met, you took the time to show us around, and made us feel special and we were very impressed with what we saw.

Our customers are telling us how important it is to them that their meat is home-reared, hung and packed nicely and without your expertise our business would not be thriving the way it is, in fact right now, we have more customers than meat!

We are looking forward to striding into the New Year and hope our association with Mainstream is a long and happy one.

Kind regards
Dave Hunt & Sarah Bexon
Manor Farm Fold, Chesterfield Road.
Oakerthorpe, ALFRETON, Derbyshire DE55 7LP

Mainstream
International Foods

Stonebroom Industrial Estate
Stonebroom
Alfreton
Derbyshire DE55 6LQ
Telephone: 01773 591177
Fax: 01773 591178
www.mainstreamfoods.co.uk

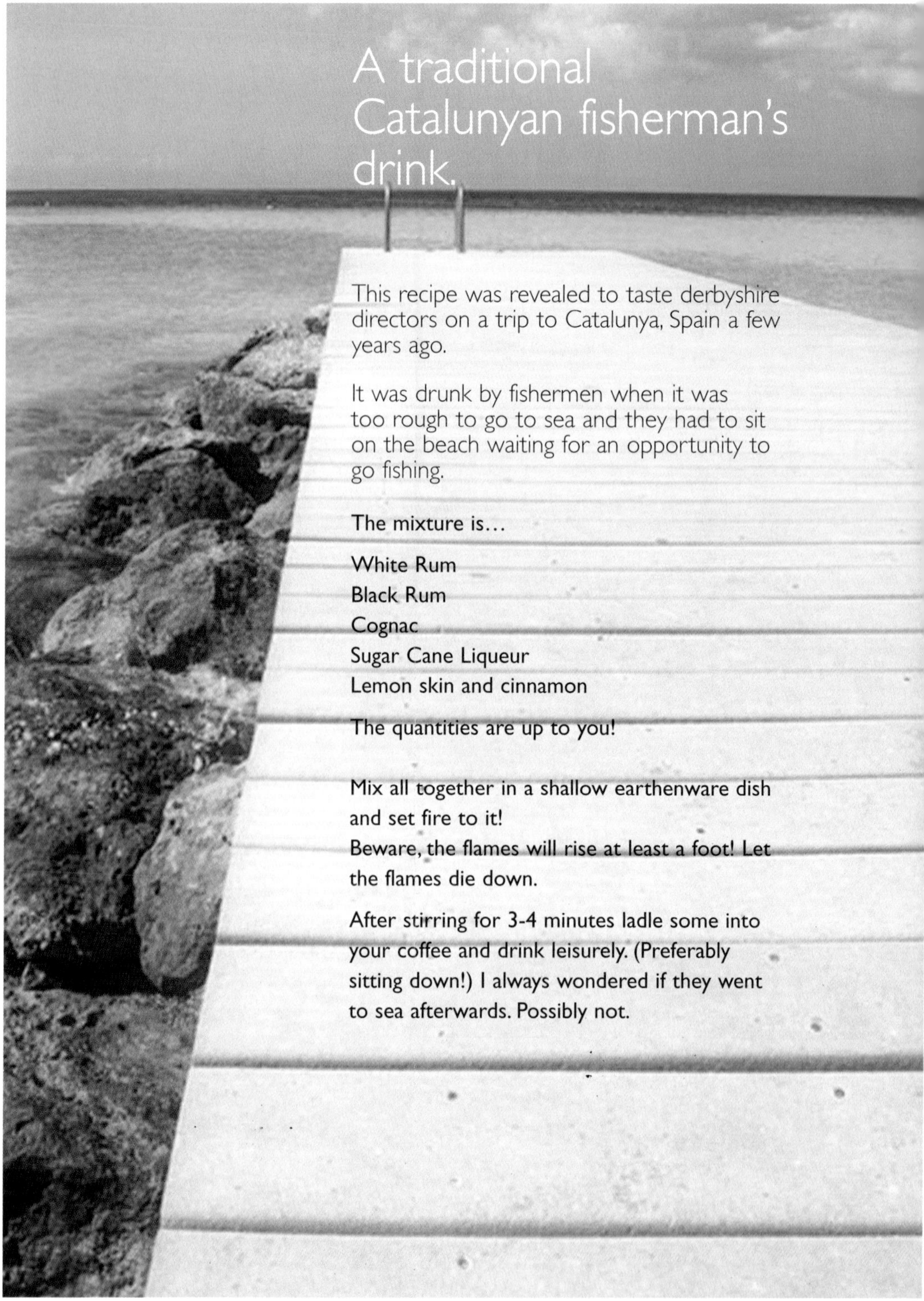

A traditional Catalunyan fisherman's drink.

This recipe was revealed to taste derbyshire directors on a trip to Catalunya, Spain a few years ago.

It was drunk by fishermen when it was too rough to go to sea and they had to sit on the beach waiting for an opportunity to go fishing.

The mixture is...

White Rum
Black Rum
Cognac
Sugar Cane Liqueur
Lemon skin and cinnamon

The quantities are up to you!

Mix all together in a shallow earthenware dish and set fire to it!
Beware, the flames will rise at least a foot! Let the flames die down.

After stirring for 3-4 minutes ladle some into your coffee and drink leisurely. (Preferably sitting down!) I always wondered if they went to sea afterwards. Possibly not.

Purveyor of Fine Foods
Lime Tree Pantry   The Bay Tree   Patchwork Paté
Burts Chips   Duchy Originals   James White
Green & Blacks Organic   The Curry Sauce Co.

Delightful food choice

at Anderson's Delicatessen,
Blind Lane, Derby.

Buckingham's
is finished!

After seven years and having overseen, as well as undertaken, the task of renovating the previously run-down property, the Buckingham family now own and operate a multi-award-winning hotel and restaurant, where the watchword is 'quality'.

Buckingham's offer a wide range of dining options
- Informal dining in the Clowns Conservatory Restaurant
- The ultimate dining experience in The Restaurant With One Table
- Cookery Courses with Master Chef Nick Buckingham
- Outside Catering, be it a small party in your own home or a large celebration.

Whatever your culinary needs Buckingham's can cater for it! For further information - visit their website www.buckinghams-table.com or ring 01246 201041

Master Chef Nick Buckingham's Cookery Courses

Ever wanted to cook like a Master Chef... here is your chance. Now, award-winning chef, Nick Buckingham now allows guests to join him in his kitchen, to share in the preparation of one of the meals he offers at his one-table restaurant in Chesterfield.

"I've always liked the idea of inviting people into my own home, where I cook, serve and entertain my guests around the dinner table," says Nick, who now lets anyone who has booked a meal in Buckingham's Restaurant come and learn, and help in the preparation of that evening's meal.

The courses are not just about following a recipe; you will be taught the techniques that will give you the confidence and ability to create your own fabulous culinary creations at home. Of course, you'll also be putting together some delicious dishes in the process and enjoying some fantastic meals.

Cookery Course and Dine in The Restaurant With One Table

The aim of the cookery course is to discuss, plan, buy ingredients and cook a meal to be served that night in 'The Famous Restaurant with One Table'. The day starts at 10.00am and approximately finishes at 4.30pm and then return for 8.00pm to dine in The Restaurant With One Table.

The cost is £250.00 per person (the prices include a lunch, refreshments, a chef's apron and recipes.) excludes the cost of the meal in The Restaurant With One Table

Cookery Course on a Specific Subject

The aim of the cookery course is to learn about a specific subject. The different subjects are Basics, Bread, Vegetables, Vegetarian, Stocks and Sauces, Pasta, Canapés, Desserts, Meat, Fish and Shellfish. The day starts at 10.00am and approximately finishes at 3.00pm

The cost is from £160.00 to £310.00 per person (the prices include a lunch, refreshments, a chef's apron and recipes.)

Proprietor: Nick Buckingham
Buckingham's Hotel and The Restaurant With One Table
85 Newbold Rd, Newbold, Chesterfield, Derbyshire S41 7PU
Telephone: 01246 201041 Fax: 01246 550059
Email: info@buckinghams-table.com
Website: www.buckinghams-table.com

Robert Walker
Peak District Dairies

At his farm near Tideswell in the north o the county, Robert has been milking his herd o dairy cattle to supply the local population wit fresh milk, butter, cream and eggs.

Having built up a very impressive milk round which includes some of the finest hotels, restaurants and farm shops, he has now built an Ice Cream Factory on his farm to supply the county's retail outlets. Using his excellent butter, milk and cream, Robert has introduced a range of flavours which include toffee, strawberry, vanilla and chocolate. These mouth watering ices are available in Derbyshire now.

Look out for The Peak District Dairy Logo on all Robert's products.

Robert's butter is the traditional deep yellow variety with an exquisite taste and texture, perfect for that slice of newly baked fresh bread and fresh strawberry jam.

Derbyshire producers

There is no better way of getting the true taste of Derbyshire than by paying a visit to the local

farmers
markets
and
farm shops

Derbyshire is blessed with quality Farmers markets including the very popular markets at Buxton, Bakewell, Derby, Belper Matlock and The Railway at Shottle near Belper.

Each of these markets gives the visitor access to locally produced seasonal food and drink.

Country markets are regular events in the county, taking place in the major towns including Bakewell, Buxton, Chesterfield, Hope Valley, and Matlock.

Along with these fantastic markets we have many fine quality farm shops selling locally grown produce including Meat, Beer, Fruit and Vegetables, Bread, Milk Cream, Butter, Ice Cream, Cheese and Chocolates, to name but a few.

Whilst many of the shops are simple affairs, one of the best known is Chatsworth Farm Shop, selling a vast range of products. Visitors from all over the country visit Chatsworth to experience the many delicacies on sale in the Peak district.

Design ICON

Most people associate the name Aga with good food and fine living. And although it's often thought of as quintessentially British, the Aga actually began life in Sweden. The celebrated cooker found in 750,000 households worldwide was invented by Dr Gustav Dalén, a blind Nobel Prize-winning physicist. Appaled that his wife and their maid had to constantly tend to their old-fashioned range, Dalén set out to design a modern cooker that would look after itself. It's unlikely Dalén could have predicted that his invention would go on to be widely acclaimed as a design icon, but it has. In the year 2000, the BBC published a retrospective of the 20th Century highlighting what it considered to be the top three design icons: first was the Coca-Cola® contour bottle, second was the VW™ Bug and third was the Aga cooker.

Over the last 80 years Aga has built on that iconic design, creating new products for the day's needs.

Additions to the Aga family like dual fuel and electric cooking products, as well as refrigeration, have brought us a long way from Dalen's first cooker in 1922, but close to our heritage

Whether it's their traditional radiant heat cookers or more conventional dual fuel and electric ranges, they have a model to suit your need for performance and your desire for style.

The classic 4-oven Aga cooker is the flagship of the Aga line. Based on a proven design of more than 80 years, the 4-oven Aga provides a truly unique and rewarding cooking experience. With 4 radiant-heat ovens, two hotplates and a warming plate this Aga has unmatched flexibility and cooking capabilities. Contact The Aga Shop, 23 Queen Street, Derby.

Pictured is the Four Oven Cooker - Gas Model

Oyster from Denby

New! Denby Oyster and Oyster Strands, designed for those who love chic! Clean, crisp with a modern twist it's perfect for morning coffee or afternoon tea, whatever the dining occasion Denby Oyster will be the talk of the table.

Anyone who owns Denby will tell you how versatile it is and how good it feels. Every piece has been designed for cooking, serving and eating food – from the 'gravy rim' on our plates to the space on our saucers for biscuits.

Their tableware is made for real food, not just for show. It's for sharing, for fingers, for chopsticks, for barbeques, for kitchens… you choose.

Denby

Discover

Royal Crown Derby

Renowned for 250 years for the manufacture of lightly potted and exquisitely decorated porcelain and bone china, Royal Crown Derby is synonymous with superlative quality and distinctive productions - including tableware, giftware and the paperweights and miniatures that are highly collectable today.

Tastes and fashions may change but the decorative and artistic skills that make their wares stand out are as popular today as they have ever been.

Discover the everlasting appeal of the myriad shapes and designs that have evolved over two and a half centuries at Royal Crown Derby.

To view the range call at their showroom on Osmaston Road, Derby or visit their web site www.royalcrownderby.co.uk

The Royal Crown Derby Porcelain Company is a privately owned Limited Company. It employs about 300 people and manufactures the highest quality English Fine Bone China at its factory on a four and a half acre site on Osmaston Road, in Derby, England.

The Company produces bone china tableware, giftware and collectables, for sale primarily in china and glass retailers and department stores, both in the UK and overseas.

The Company also runs a popular Visitor Centre at Osmaston Road, providing factory tours, demonstrations, museum, factory shop and restaurant.

The present factory was established in 1878 but the business traces its origins to the original factory which was set up in Nottingham Road in about 1750. Queen Victoria granted permission to include the title "Royal" in the company name in 1890.

Food looks
so much better
on fine tableware

St Clements Bakery
Love is all you knead

Bread is the staple food of many cultures. From a few simple ingredients the most nutritious, versatile or exotic food can be created. Needing no crockery or cutlery bread is truly a meal in itself - to hit the spot at breakfast time or share with friends over dinner.

Neil and Sue Chatterton began their bakery business, St Clements, some ten years ago. They swapped their London chef skills and relocated 'up North', Neil being a Yorkshire lad at heart.

Using their cookery skills and passion for food they chose to specialise in baking bread. Bread has become extremely cosmopolitan. Due to travel and the media bread, is no longer available as just white or brown, here you can choose from hand crafted delights such as French Campagrain, naturally leavened sourdough, authentic Italian Ciabatta, fruited Rye and savoury Pain rustique. Included are a large selection of savoury pies, quiches, pastries and homemade style cakes. You can easily plan your weekly menu around their goods.

All are lovingly manufactured by a team of four at their bakery workshop in Chesterfield. The upturn in customer demand for back to basics, additive and preservative free goods is proving so popular they are actively looking for a suitable retail outlet.

DERBYSHIRE SMOKERY
producers of a wide variety of
Smoked Fish and Meat products,
Flagg, near Buxton.

Alan Hobson and Ian Jennings with an impressive background in the restaurant and butchery trade over many years, are now producing aromatic and fragrant smoked goodies such as Hot Smoked Duck, locally sourced chicken along with Roast Ham, Trout, Hot and Cold Smoked Salmon, Cornish Mackerel, Haddock, Prawns and a selection of home made pasties and fish cakes prepared with care into a range of hot and cold smoked products.

They use a coarse sea salt for curing and a special herb and spice seasoning before smoking the products over a variety of natural hard wood chippings, each chosen to complement and enhance the different types of meat. Alder is used for mackerel and cold smoked salmon, oak for roast ham, hickory for chicken and duck, and a special blend for hot smoked salmon.

They only use natural products and most are suitable for people that are on a gluten free diet.

You can find the Derbyshire Smokery products at the Chatsworth Farm Shop, Ibbotsons Village Store Ashford in the Water, Smiths Deli Ashbourne, Denby Pottery, Amberside Farm Shop Pentrich Lane End. Alternatively, catch them at Bakewell, Belper, Buxton, Matlock, Castleton, Sheffield, Birmingham, Lichfield, Ashton, farmers markets and local food fayres.

REAL FARM FRESH FOOD
Amberside Farm Shop

Located in the heart of the Amber Valley, a mile from Ripley, is a family run business that supplies the best in local, organic and naturally produced food. Incredibly, the business has been going for over 20 years, originally as seasonal farm gate sales selling directly from growers, and recently expanding into the beautifully renovated surroundings of a converted stable next to the River Amber.

Amberside Farm Shop sets out to give a fairer deal for both customers and farmers alike. Run by Iain and Marianne Sterland, they aim to stock the highest quality food produced as locally as possible, thus reducing food miles and supporting independent food producers. In fact it was this desperation in finding an alternative to the big supermarkets that has led to the Farm Shop being the success it is today. "In the beginning we started selling organically produced fruit and vegetables, as it was so difficult to buy locally at a reasonable price. Historically, Derbyshire is not a vegetable growing county, so we have had to source a lot from farms in Lincolnshire and further afield. We are delighted that more Derbyshire farmers are expanding their ranges, and many are now growing produce directly for us."

The shop offers a wide selection of organic vegetables and fruit, Derbyshire reared meats and sausages, produce from The Derbyshire Smokery, a wide selection of ready to eat food from Robin Maycock and Lime Tree Pantry, delicious cakes from Tasty Treats, Thaymar ice creams, bread from Allsops, Derbyshire honey from Littleover Apiaries, Suma co-operative produce, Ecover cleaning products, skincare from Weleda and much more.

Whilst sourcing locally is obviously very important to them, Iain and Marianne sell mainly organic products that are produced responsibly using environmentally sustainable farming methods. "We won't compromise on quality or

taste. We don't deal with the big guys, and we don't stock anything we wouldn't eat ourselves. We want to champion real food heroes. We also stock a wide variety of great foods which aren't available locally, including black puddings and haggis from the Outer Hebrides, olive oil from Spain, fairly traded coffee and chocolate."

"Our customers like us because we have the variety of produce that a Farmers Market has but under one roof. We are easy to find, you can park directly outside, and we offer a friendly service. We are open during the week and our customers can buy their favourites from us, rather than wait for the market which is only once a month. We are convenient and many customers have become friends. We aim to build long lasting relationships with both our customers and suppliers."

Amberside Farm Shop has the authenticity of a Farmers Market five days a week. It is easy to find, convenient and friendly, and directly supports local farmers and independents to offer a real choice.

For opening times and further information contact Iain and Marianne on 01773 512211 at Amberside Farm Shop, Pentrich Lane End, near Ripley, Derbyshire, DE5 3RH

Award Winning
Amber Ales

Established in 2006, Amber Ales is the creation of Peter & Jayn Hounsell. Eponymously named after the Amber Valley in which it is located, the five barrel plant can produce over 5000 pints of beer a week and is already making its mark with its award winning ales and demand outstripping supply.

The brewery produces 'modern' real ales, that are full of flavour but follow time honoured traditional methods of production. Peter, inspired by the American Micros with their hop charged 'new' ales, tells us "We aim to make a difference with our beer. The real ale market is dominated by heavy, worthy ales which are very bland in flavour and can be either too bitter or too sweet. At the other end of the scale you get the characterless mass produced 'Euro' lagers - our beers are refreshingly lighter, with a better balance of hop flavours and aromas rather than just bitterness and we are finding these appeal to a wider audience, not just the traditional real ale drinkers."

The combination of enjoying the odd pint or two and being a Chemical Engineer by profession has proved to be a great asset, and Peter has spent a good many years perfecting his recipes, honing the flavours before venturing to make his beer on a commercial scale. After studying at Sunderland University's Brewlab, Peter established the brewery in Hammersmith, Ripley and his first brew 'Amber Pale' was awarded 'Beer of the Festival' by Tamworth CAMRA, relegating the Champion Beer of Great Britain into second place! Further awards have followed, as has the demand for Amber Ales across the region.

Amber Ales has four core beers: Amber Pale (4.4% abv), Amber Blond (3.6% abv), Original Stout (4.0% abv) and the impressive Imperial Pale Ale (6.5% abv), plus a number of seasonal additions. Each beer is designed to complement food, and is supplied with tasting notes. It is available in cask and as bottle conditioned, the bottle equivalent of a draught real ale. All are 'live beers', naturally carbonated and undergoing a secondary fermentation in the bottle or cask, allowing the flavours to mature and develop over time. Each beer is brewed by hand and made with only natural ingredients – hops, barley, yeast and of course water, with no additional chemicals nor preservatives. The flavours are allowed to develop through an unforced fermentation process, a beer made in this way is like a fine wine, maturing and developing over time, as far removed from the mass production of the large 'chemical' brewers as it could possibly be.

For further information Amber Ales can be contacted at PO Box 7277, Ripley, Derbyshire, DE5 4AP. Telephone: 01773 512864

GULLIVER'S
Paté

Strange heading you may think, but read on and you will find out its significance. On a superbly warm clear and sunny Tuesday, I wandered my way over Beeley Moor to embark on, what for me, was a labour of love, making paté. I love paté in all its forms, smooth or rough, if it's on the menu, I order it. Yes, possibly an old stick-in-the-mud, but to me it starts my meal off in a way that I enjoy. So, to be able to go and be involved in the making of paté was a little dream come true. Especially as the end result would be tasting it!

Andre Birkitt, the manager of Chatsworth Farm Shop had agreed to allow us into his kitchens to see, and help, in the making of their speciality patés. On arrival John and I were greeted by David Nicklin, Head Chef at Chatsworth Farm Shop, who informed us of the morning's proceedings whilst I was changing into my chef's clothing. The most important ingredient came next, coffee, and then onto work. All the prep work had taken place earlier on in the morning as they are early starters, with the ingredients laid out in preparation for our arrival. We immediately confused David with our questions and general lack of knowledge with regards to the process of making paté' and we set off on the wrong recipe! David quickly made a management decision and we were back on track.

My first job was to start stirring, something I am good at! I was taken to a very large stove, on which was a very large pot and given a very large paddle, Kontiki style. 'Stir that', said David 'and keep an eye on it for the next half an hour whilst we also prepare for the next paté'. We were making two patés at the same time, Darling Budds and Andre's Pate', which confused me and I immediately forgot

which was which and just kept my head down and carefully followed David's instructions. Fortunately he knew exactly where we were.

At this time of year there are on average 5 different Patés on sale at Chatsworth Farm Shop, rising later in the year to 9. The ingredients range from chicken liver, today's recipe, duck, pork and a vegetarian one too. Some are topped with bacon, others with butter and parsley and so on. These variations ensure that their regular customers can enjoy a variety of tastes year round.

Whilst we were busy doing our prep work, there were other recipes being accomplished around us, one individual was making the most exotic quiches which included mozzarella and peppers, game pies filled with venison etc, pork pies, sausage rolls and a host of things in the bakery were all on the go and all needing co-ordinating. All the people involved knew exactly their weekly tasks and were all just beavering away to accomplish them with minimum fuss. Their only problem was us getting in the way. I seemed to be in the wrong spot on more than one

occasion, hearing a constant 'excuse me' as someone else keen to do their job needed to get by.

It was now time to get my gloves on as the Darling Budd's paté has to be mixed by hand because this is a rough pate and the ingredients don't need crushing, but tenderly mixing in to avoid a bitter taste. The smooth paté was mixed in a very large mixer with huge adjustable blades to get right to the bottom of the bowl. The consistency became very fine. Once all the ingredients were mixed, it was time to put the patés in their dishes, which I was entrusted with after a bit of training. You may think that this is an easy task. Well yes it is but, as a novice I was painfully slow, whilst trying to be accurate and drop not a bit. With the smooth pate all done

and into their containers, it was onto the Darling Budds, which needed not only the paté in the containers, but topping off with bacon. The bacon needed laying on the top, trimming and then tucking down the sides before being sealed and put into a so large refrigerator, that you can walk around in. David showed us how things were stored for maximum freshness and how all things are dated so that everything that appears on the counters is of top quality and extremely fresh. We watched, the quiches grew in the large ovens which were next to the large steam ovens and the large chiller.

Having done our work, it was time for the tasting. At last! We went into the demonstration room with coffee, fresh bread and a selection of paté to taste. In a relaxed atmosphere away from the bustle of the kitchen David explained how some of the paté recipes had come about, and constantly change. Now, the title of the article. Having finished at Chatsworth I went home and felt like Gulliver. There in our kitchen was a small oven and a small mixer with a small ladle in a small bowl! Yes I was in Lilliput! Not really - but you know what I mean. All morning everything had been large, but then with the success of Chatsworth Farm Shop they need to be to able cope with the vast demand on their produce. As we ventured from the kitchen towards the end of the morning, the queues at the tills were starting to form, and the fresh bread showing signs of being snapped up.

My thanks to all at Chatsworth Farm Shop for their patience and hospitality. I had a super morning.   G.P.

Darling Budd Terrine

Mrs Budd, whose recipe this is, is a dear friend of the Dowager Duchess of Devonshire.

Preparation time: 20 mins
Cooking time: 1¼hrs
Oven temperature: 170˚C

Ingredients
625g Minced Pork
300g Chicken Livers, trimmed
300g Bacon, minced or finely chopped
300g 8/10 rashers Streaky Bacon
25g Butter
1 Clove Garlic, crushed
2.5g or app 12 Juniper Berries (lightly crushed)
1.25g Thyme
80ml Red Wine
Salt & Pepper

Method
1. Preheat the oven to 170˚C/325˚F, gas mark 3.
2. Heat the butter and fry together the minced bacon and garlic.
3. In a mixing bowl, combine the minced pork, thyme, juniper berries, red wine and salt and pepper.
4. When the bacon is cooked, add to the pork mixture.
5. To the mixture add the chicken livers and mix slowly to avoid crushing them.
6. Place in a terrine and cover with streaky bacon.
7. Cover with foil and stand in a roasting tin half filled with hot water and bake for 1¼ hours at 170˚C/325˚F, gas mark 3, (or until the core temperature is 80˚C. Test this with a meat thermometer).
8. Cool, then refrigerate.
9. Serve with Cumberland sauce and crusty bread.

And now
the recipes

To
begin with…

Bruschetta
with Rocksalt and Rosemary

Preparation time: 5 mins
Cooking time: 25 mins
Oven temperature: 225°C

Ingredients
750g Strong plain white flour
2 tbsps easy blend yeast
Salt
3 tbsp Caster Sugar
11 fl oz Water
3 tbsp Olive Oil
Rock Salt
Sprigs of Fresh Rosemary

Method

1. Using a bread maker, follow the instructions for ordinary white bread or for oil bread. They should be similar quantities to the above list. Remove from the machine just after the final rising.

2. Place the dough on a floured board and knead into a ball. Now stretch and pull this into an oblong to fit a greased large shallow baking tin.

3. Press holes into the dough using your fingertips, drizzle oil over and allow to fill the hollows.
   Sprinkle with rock salt and sprigs of rosemary.

4. Bake in the centre of a hot oven 225°C for about 25 minutes. Serve warm with balsamic vinegar and oil and a selection of olives.

Asparagus Spears in Garlic Butter

Preparation time: 5 mins
Cooking time: 7 mins

Ingredients
Bunch of fresh asparagus
5ml (a drizzle) lemon infused Oil
A cube of butter
3 cloves of garlic, finely chopped
Salt and pepper

Method
1. Wash the asparagus. Trim any thick stalks.
2. Heat the oil and butter in a pan and cook the asparagus for 5 minutes, turning regularly.
3. Add the crushed garlic and cook for a further 2 minutes.
4. Serve and season with salt and pepper. Garnish with fresh parsley and scatter a little of the chopped garlic on top.

Pesto and Cheese Catherine Wheels

Preparation time: 10 mins
Cooking time: 25 mins
Oven temperature: 200˚C

This is a simple to make, tasty canapé, ideal to serve to guests with drinks before a meal or a barbeque.

Ingredients
Ready made rolled puff pastry
4oz cheddar cheese
1 jar of red pesto

Method
1. Unroll the puff pastry. Spread the pesto evenly over the pastry.
2. Grate the cheese and spread on top of the pesto. Using the cellophane the puff pastry is in, role tightly lengthways.
3. Cut into slices about 1cm thick and arrange on a baking sheet covered in greased proof paper.
4. Bake in a hot oven 200 C for about 25 minutes.
5. Remove from the tray and allow to cool on a cooling rack.

For variations use your imagination and create your own favourite fillings.
Marmite and Cheshire cheese works well.

Basil, Tomato and Garlic Stick

Preparation time: 10 mins
Cooking time: 10 mins

Ingredients
1 white French bread stick
2 plum tomatoes
1 clove garlic
Bunch basil
Quality Italian extra virgin
olive oil

1. Slice bread stick acutely diagonal to make as long a slice as possible.
2. Immerse tomatoes in a bowl of hot water to remove the skin, and dice.
3. Wash and tear basil.
4. Peel a clove of garlic.

5. Generously drizzle the oil on one side of the bread and place under a hot grill until golden brown, then rub the clove of garlic on half the slices and decorate each with a basil leaf.
6. On the remaining half of the slices, layer with the plum tomatoes, drizzle with a little olive oil. Arrange on a plate and place in the middle of the table.

Smoked Venison
in a creamy avocado sauce

Preparation time: 15 mins

Ingredients
100g (4oz) cold Cooked
Smoked Venison from
specialist delicatessen
1 Peeled and stoned
Avocado, roughly chopped
$1/2$ tbsp lemon juice
1 glove of garlic crushed
1 tbsp tomato puree
50g (2oz) soft full fat cheese
50g (2oz) fromage frais
Tabasco Sauce

Method
1. Place the cold, smoked
   venison either whole or
   sliced on a serving plate
2. Mix all the remaining
   ingredients together and
   season to taste with a few
   drops of Tabasco sauce.

Serve with a mixed salad and
the venison garnished with
parsley and lemon.

Sauté Apple and Pear Salad with warm cheese

Preparation time: 25 mins
Cooking time: 20 mins

Ingredients
2 slices of white bread
1 tablespoon of olive oil
Mixed leaf green salad
1 green pear
1 red apple
2oz walnut pieces
1 tablespoon ground nut oil
1oz butter
200 gm tub of crème fraiche
4oz dolce latte, blue creamy cheese
Yolk of 1 egg

Method
1. First cut the crusts of bread to leave squares. Cut into small cubes.
2. Put oil into the bowl and toss the bread cubes well in the oil.
3. Spread onto a non-stick tray without cubes touching and bake for approx 10 minutes in a pre-heated oven, 180˚C.
4. Put to one side (or can be stored in an air tight tub when cold). Wash the salad leaves.
5. Wash, quarter and core the apple and pear. Half each piece again to make eighths. Heat ground nut oil to medium heat in a heavy based pan, add walnuts and keep them moving about in the pan for 2 minutes then remove and drain onto kitchen paper.
6. Add butter to pan, again on medium heat and add fruit when the butter has melted. Turn and cook until golden brown.
7. In a small saucepan, warm the crème fraiche adding cubes of the dolce latte and stir until it melts into the cream. Separate the yoke of an egg and add, whisking and simmer gently for 3 or 4 minutes until the sauce coates the back of a wooden spoon.
8. Pile the green leaves in the centre of the pate, arrange apples and pears and sprinkle croutons and walnuts on. Pour the warm cheese dressing all over the salad and serve quickly.

Goats Cheese Filo Parcels

Preparation time: 15 mins
Cooking time: 20 mins
Oven temperature: 180°C

Ingredients
Ready made filo pastry
2oz melted butter
4 individual circular goats
cheeses
Mixed green leaf salad
4 tablespoons Balsamic
Vinegar
1 tablespoon olive oil
2 teaspoons Brown Sugar

Method
1. Prepare the ingredients and grease a baking sheet before you begin as the filo dries out quickly.
2. Put the first sheet of filo on your work area and brush with melted butter. Lay the 2nd layer on top but running the other way forming a cross, brush with melted butter.
3. Put the goats cheese in the middle, reduce the filo by trimming 1 inch off each length. Gather up the filo roughly, to form a parcel and brush with melted butter. Place on a baking sheet and bake for 20 minutes 180 C.
4. Put Balsamic vinegar in a saucepan with the sugar and simmer for 10 minutes to reduce, add oil. Drizzle around the plate. Serve with green salad and small, vine tomatoes.

and now
to **follow**

Roast Crown of Lamb

Preparation time: 15 mins
Cooking time: 45 mins
(medium Rare)

Ingredients
2 racks of lamb, trimmed of
fat, assembled into a crown
and tied (6 ribs each rack)*
$^1/_4$ cup olive oil
2 tablespoon of lemon juice
1 teaspoon of coarse salt
$^1/_2$ teaspoon black pepper
Stuffing
Quality ready made stuffing
100g (4oz) dried apricots

Pre heat oven to 240°C

Method
1. Create a marinade using
   the lemon juice, olive oil,
   salt and pepper. Baste the
   marinade onto the lamb
   racks.
2. Make up the stuffing as
   per the instructions on the
   packet, add the chopped
   apricots and allow to
   stand for 10 minutes.
3. Fill the centre of the
   crown with the stuffing,
   pressing it down gently.
4. Cover the bones at the
   top with foil to prevent
   burning.

5. Place in a shallow
   roasting pan and bake for
   30 minutes.
6. Reduce the heat to 190C.
   Baste the lamb again
7. Allow to cook an
   additional 20-35 minutes.
   This will now be medium
   rare. Add an extra five
   minute cooking time and
   check again until it is
   cooked to your liking.

Serve with a selection of
roasted root vegetables.
Place paper crown on tips
before serving.

*A quality butcher will do all
the work for you here, and
prepare a nice looking crown.

Spinach and Mozzerella Pancakes

Preparation time: 20 mins
Cooking time: 35 mins
Oven temperature: 180-190°C

Ingredients
Ready made savoury pancakes
450g (1lb) small leaf spinach
25g (1oz) butter
2 balls of mozzarella
Whole Nutmeg
Plum tomatoes, diced
Salt and Pepper
Tub of crème fraiche
1 Egg
Parmesan
Pine Nuts

Method

1. Melt the butter in a large pan and wilt down the spinach with the lid on.
2. Drain the mozzarella and dice.
3. Mix in a bowl with the tomatoes, drain the spinach and add to the bowl, season. Add grated fresh nutmeg. Mix together and place spoonfuls down the centre of each pancake (should make between 4 and 6).
4. Roll up and place in oven proof dish.
5. Whisk the yolk of one egg in a bowl. Simmer gently the crème fraiche for 3 or 4 minutes and add the egg, cooking for a further 2 minutes
6. Pour over the pancakes. Sprinkle generously with parmesan and pine nuts bake at 200°C for 30 minutes.

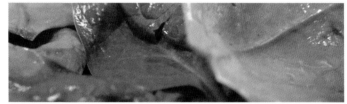

Baked Haddock
with Cheesy Crunch Topping

Preparation time: 20 mins
Cooking time: 35 mins
Oven temperature: 190°C

Ingredients
680g (1½ lb) Haddock Fillets, skinless
3 tbsp Butter
6 Spring Onions, thinly sliced
1 tbsp Fresh Chopped Parsley
2 - 3 tbsp finely diced Red Bell Pepper or Roasted Red Bell Pepper, diced
⅔ Cups Crushed Small White Cheddar Cheese Crackers
⅓ Cup Bread-crumbs, plain or seasoned
2 - 3 tbsp Single Cream
Salt and Pepper
Herb seasoning blend

Method
1. Place haddock fillets, in a buttered baking dish.
2. In a sauté or frying pan, heat the butter over a medium heat, add the spring onions, pepper and cook until soft.
3. Add the parsley, cracker crumbs, bread crumbs and stir.
4. Add the cream to moisten.
5. Season the haddock with salt, pepper and herbs. Cover with the crumb mixture.
6. Bake for 25 minutes at 190°C.

Bacon Supper Snack

Preparation time: 10 mins
Cooking time: 35-40 mins
Oven temperature: 175°C

Ingredients
8 Slices of thickly cut baked ham
450g (1lb) Tin of tomatoes
Knob of butter
57g (2 oz) mushrooms, sliced thinly
85g (3 oz) white breadcrumbs
$\frac{1}{2}$ tsp mixed herbs
1 egg
Salt and pepper

Method
1. Melt the butter in a saucepan and add the sliced mushrooms, cook for 2 minutes.
2. Add the breadcrumbs, salt pepper and herbs.
3. Beat the egg and add enough to bind the mixture.
4. Lay out the gammon slices and divide the mixture equally on them. Roll up and place in a buttered baking dish. Place under a hot grill and cook for around 5 minutes.
5. Press the tomatoes through a sieve, place in a saucepan and bring to the boil, pour over the gammon and cook at 175°C gas mark 3 for 30 minutes.

Serve with potatoes or a green salad.

Roasted Brussel Sprouts
with apples and onions

Preparation time: 10 mins
Cooking time: 35 mins
Oven temperature: 220°C

Ingredients
2 tbsp Olive Oil
2 tbsp Butter
450g (1 lb) Brussel Sprouts, washed, trimmed and halved
3 Granny Smith Apples, peeled, cored and cut into wedges
1 Red Onion, peeled and cut into wedges
1 tsp Ground Pepper
Half a lemon
6 Thyme Sprigs
1 Cup Apple Cider

Method
1. Preheat the oven to 220°C
2. Melt the butter and olive oil in a roasting pan.
3. Add the sprouts, apples and onion, season with salt, pepper and lemon juice. Stir to ensure that everything is coated in the butter and oil. Scatter the thyme sprigs among the sprouts
4. Roast in the oven until the vegetables are tender, about 30 minutes.
5. Remove the vegetables, discarding the thyme sprigs, and place in a serving dish and keep warm.
6. Place the roasting pan on a medium heat and add the apple cider to the remaining juices and reduce slightly.
7. Pour the reduced sauce over the vegetables and serve

This reciepe has been supplied and created by head chef, Will Frankgate and is on the menu at The New Highwayman, Eastmoor, Chesterfield.

21 day matured Derbyshire
Fillet of Beef with local
Hartington Stilton Rarebit and a tawny port glaze

Ingredients
4x6oz Fillet steaks
Olive oil
Salt & freshly ground pepper
The Glaze
568ml Fresh beef stock (good quality)
20g Cold butter
200ml Tawny port
Sprig of thyme
The Rarebit
200g Grated Stilton
3 Eggs
6 heaped Tablespoons of fresh breadcrumbs
1 Table spoon English mustard
1 Tablespoon Worcester sauce
60ml Whole milk
100ml Bitter
1 Tablespoon chopped parsley
Salt & Pepper

Method
1. Grate the Stilton into a large mixing bowl, add the eggs, breadcrumbs, bitter, milk, mustard, Worcester sauce, parsley, salt & pepper & mix together.
2. Pan fry the fillets, season with salt & pepper & olive oil. Pan fry until sealed on all sides, finish off in the oven for 4-5 mins at 200˚C, then leave to rest for 5 mins wrapped in foil.
3. In the same pan, using a metal egg ring or mould, spoon approx 4-5 tablespoons of the rarebit mixture into it and cook on both sides until golden brown. Remove from the pan & keep hot.

4. For the glaze, put 200ml port in a saucepan, reduce until the alcohol has evaporated. Add the stock & reduce by half. Whisk in the cold butter and a sprig of thyme.

To serve
Place the fillet on a dinner plate, sit the rarebit on top of the fillet, and put a sprig of thyme on top of the rarebit and spoon over the glaze. Serve with seasonal vegetables or alternatively a nice fresh mixed leaf salad.

Steak
with roasted red pepper coulis

Preparation time: 15 mins
Cooking time: 7 mins

Ingredients
4 Boneless Beef Tenderloin
Steaks
$\frac{1}{2}$ tsp Black Pepper
Small clove of grated garlic
$\frac{1}{2}$ tsp Salt
200g (7oz) Jar of Roasted
Red Peppers
Oil for coating frying pan

Method
1. Drain the peppers, saving a few and some of the liquid, rinse and pat dry the peppers.
2. Finely dice the peppers, with the garlic and add a pinch of salt. Rub both sides of the steaks with this mixture.
3. Heat the oil in a frying pan pan, add the steaks and cook for about 2 - 3

minutes each side.
4. Place the remaining peppers and some of the liquid with a pinch of salt in a blender and puree until smooth. If the mixture is too firm add some more of the pepper liquid.
5. To serve: pour some of the red pepper coulis onto a plate and place the steak on top.

Pad Thai

Kaeng Kiew Wan Moo

Pad Thai Thai stir-fried rice noodles

Preparation time: 10 mins
Cooking time: 10 mins

Ingredients
500g (1lb 2oz) thin rice
noodles
1 cup beansprouts
½ cup cut spring onion
1 tbsp chopped red onion
1 tbsp fried cubed bean curd
1 tbsp chopped pickled
turnip
1 fresh egg
1 tbsp vegetable oil

Seasoning
2 tbsp tamarind sauce
1 tbsp palm sugar
1 tbsp fish sauce
½ tsp dark soy sauce

Condiments
Ground peanuts
Fresh lime wedges

Method
1. Heat vegetable oil in a wok
   on medium heat
2. Fry chopped onions until
   soft
3. Add egg until cooked
4. Add rice noodles and
   cook until soft
5. Add tamarind sauce and
   black soy sauce
6. Add bean curd and
   pickled turnip
7. Mix all ingredients
   together
8. Remove from the heat,
   add spring onion and
   beansprouts
9. Serve with condiments
   and some fresh
   beansprouts

These recipes
have been kindly
supplied by the
chefs of
Siam Corner
Thai Village
Derby.

Kaeng Kiew Wan Moo
Thai green pork curry

Preperation time:
Cooking time:
Serves 4

Ingredients
2 tbsp thai green curry paste
500g (1lb 2oz) sliced pork
1 tin coconut milk
1 aubergine, chop in chunks
1 fresh medium size red and 1
green chillie, slice
10g sweet basil leaves
1 kaffir lime leaf

Seasoning
1 tbsp fish sauce
1 tsp palm sugar

Method:
1. Heat the pan until it is
   medium hot and add half of
   the coconut milk
2. Add the curry paste and
   cook until you can smell
   the herbs
3. Add pork and the rest of
   coconut milk and bring to
   the boil
4. Add the seasoning and
   taste
5. Add chunks of aubergine
   and cook until soft
6. Add chillies, sweet basil
   and kaffir lime leaves
7. Serve with steamed rice

Chef **Rachel Green**

is renowned for her passion for food,

and her love of seasonal and local produce.

With two TV series under her belt, and a third in development, she has brought these passions together. In her first series, The Flying Cook, www.yorkshiretv.com Rachel visited food producers right across the region by helicopter, and took the ingredients home to cook in her converted barn. In her latest series, World on A Plate, to be screened in April 2007, Rachel celebrates ethnic cuisines with families living in the region, from Hindu to West Indian, from Polish to Jewish families.

Rachel is also the official Champion for Tastes of Lincolnshire www.visitlincolnshire.com and face of the East Midlands, for the taste England campaign launched by Visit Britain www.VisitBritain.org.

A farmer's daughter from Lincolnshire, her family have farmed in the county for 14 generations. She has helped lamb ewes, lifted potatoes, stripped peas from the vine and combined the wheat. "It means I have a huge respect for producers," she declares, " I know just how much hard work has gone into it!" She has cooked for 8 to 800, many times for the Royal Family, ran her own restaurant Grainthorpe Hall for several years. She cooks often on radio and television, including the BBC's first-ever interactive TV series, alongside Delia Smith, Rick Stein and Gary Rhodes.

She demonstrates regularly at the Chatsworth Farm Shop www.chatsworth.org by invitation of the Dowager Duchess of Devonshire who shares her passion for local, seasonal food, and also at the Divertimenti Cookery Theatre www.divertimenti.co.uk.

Her exuberant cookery demonstrations are much in demand all over the country - she has cooked breakfast for Terry Wogan every day for Farmhouse Breakfast Week, for the pea growers of Britain at the Royal Show, at the CLA Game Fair at Belvoir Castle, at the BBC Good Food Show. Unusually, Rachel has her own magnificent custom-built mobile cookery demonstration unit, made specially for her by the award-winning bespoke kitchen makers, Chiselwood www.chiselwood.co.uk.

She has also devised numerous recipes for all sorts of vegetables, from chicory and celeriac www.jackbuck.co.uk shallots UKShallot.com peas www.peas.org chantenay carrots www.chantenay.co.uk carrots www.britishcarrots.co.uk asparagus www.british-asparagus.co.uk and for all the major supermarkets.

Her work is featured in many publications including Hello! Fresh, You Are What You Eat, Family Circle and Love It, and taste derbyshire.

Rachel is available for:
Cookery demonstrations
Recipe development
Bespoke outside catering
Food styling and photography with award-winning photographer Michael Powell www.michaelpowell.com
Masterclasses
Private tuition
Lectures and talks

The following are three recipes are from Rachel Green's culinary repertoire.

Tempura of Jerusalem Artichokes
with garlic and lemon Aioli Makes 20

Ingredients
20 small artichokes
55g self raising flour
55g cornflour
pinch salt
Sparkling water, very well chilled
Sunflower or vegetable oil for frying

For the aioli:
4 tbsp good quality mayonnaise
4 cloves garlic
½ tbsp olive oil
Zest and juice of ½ lemon

Preheat the oven to 180°C/350°F/Gas Mark 4. Soak 20 wooden skewers in water.

To make the aioli drizzle the garlic cloves with ½ tbsp olive oil, wrap in foil and roast in the preheated oven for 20-25 minutes, until softened. Squeeze the cloves out of their skins and mix with the mayonnaise and lemon zest and juice. Season and set aside.

For the tempura batter, sift the self raising flour and cornflour into a bowl with a pinch of salt. Make a well in the centre, and add a little sparkling water. Gradually draw in the flour to make a smooth batter. Add enough water to make a batter of double cream consistency.

Peel the artichokes and skewer each one onto a soaked skewer. Heat the oil in a large, deep saucepan, until a piece of bread will take 1 minute to brown. You do not want the oil too hot or the tempura will be burnt before being cooked through. Dip each artichoke skewer into the tempura batter, making sure it is well and evenly coated, then place carefully into the hot oil, balancing the end of the skewer against the side of the pan. Cook for 3-4 minutes, until golden brown and cooked through.

Drain well on kitchen paper and serve with the roasted garlic and lemon aioli. Drizzle with soy sauce if desired.

Italian Red Chicory stuffed with Black Olives, Parmesan and Pine Nuts Serves 4 – 6

Ingredients

1 med onion, peeled and finely chopped
2 cloves garlic, finely chopped
4 tbsp olive oil
120g flat mushrooms, finely chopped
75g pine nuts
1 tbsp chopped parsley
50g black olives, finely diced
1 handful basil leaves, torn
3 tsp sundried tomato pesto
100g grated parmesan
6 heads red chicory
Sea salt and freshly ground black pepper

Dressing (optional)

1tbsp olive oil
2tsp sundried tomato pesto
2tsp red wine vinegar
Sea salt and freshly ground black pepper

Method

Fry the onion and garlic in 3 tbsp of the olive oil for approx 2 minutes until soft. Add the finely chopped mushrooms and the pine nuts and cook for a further 2 to 3 minutes. Add the chopped parsley, black olives, basil, sundried tomato pesto and parmesan, saving a handful of the parmesan to use later.

Trim the end of the chicory root then cut in half lengthways and remove the white core taking care to keep the leaves together. Place on a baking tray, season with sea salt and black pepper and brush with the remaining olive oil. Grill under a hot grill for 1 - 1½ minutes taking care not to overcook on the first grilling. Stuff each chicory half with plenty of the warm stuffing mixture and sprinkle with the remaining parmesan. Lower the grill to a medium heat and cook for 4 to 5 minutes allowing the stuffing to cook without losing the colour and texture of the chicory.

Mix the dressing ingredients together and drizzle over the stuffed chicory. Serve with crusty bread and a green salad or rice.

PER SERVING (4) 326 kcalories, 16g protein, 16g carbohydrates, 24g fat, 5g saturated fat, 10g fibre, 2g sugars, 4.08g sodium.

Nutrition – as well as the nutritional value of the Chicory this recipe contains: vitamin A and beta carotene, B complex vitamins, vitamin C, vitamin E, calcium, magnesium, manganese, selenium, iron, zinc, potassium, quercitin, allicin plus other antioxidants from the herbs and seasonings

Vegetable Tagine

with Peas, Squash, Carrots and Apricots Serves 4 – 6

Ingredients
300g frozen peas
1 onion, diced
1 kg mixed squash, sweet potato, carrots and
swede, peeled and diced into medium chunks
20 dried apricot
3 tbsp olive oil
½ tsp ground ginger
1 cinnamon stick
1 tsp cumin seeds
1 tsp ground cumin
1 tsp white pepper
Good pinch saffron soaked in 50ml warm water
2 cloves garlic, chopped and crushed
Handful fresh chopped coriander
Handful fresh chopped parsley
½ fresh chilli, chopped (optional)
4 tomatoes skinned and roughly chopped
sea salt and freshly ground black pepper

Heat the oil in a flame proof casserole dish. Soften the onion and then add the mixed vegetables. Coat well in the oil. Add the ginger, cinnamon stick, cumin seeds, ground cumin, saffron, white pepper, garlic, fresh chilli, the parsley and half of the coriander. Cook for a further two minutes then add the apricots and the tomatoes and a dash of water to produce a thick sauce. Season with sea salt and black pepper. Cover and cook over a medium heat for about 30 minutes. 5 minutes towards the end of the cooking time, add the peas. Cover and cook. Generally no additional water is required as there is sufficient liquid from the onion and tomatoes. Keep a check and add a little water if needed. Adjust the seasoning and serve with lemon couscous and garnish with the remaining coriander.

Spanish Omelette

Preparation time: 10 mins

Ingredients
3 Eggs
3 Tsp Cold Water
Salt and Pepper
40g (1$^{1}/_{2}$oz) Butter
1 Small Onion
1 tbsp Cooked Diced Potato
1 tbsp Cooked Peas

Method
1. Heat the butter in an omelette or frying pan, add the onion and cook slowly until soft.
2. Add the cooked diced potato and peas.
3. Place the eggs, water and seasoning in a bowl and whisk lightly.
4. Add the egg mixture to the vegetables in the omelette pan. Cook as plain omelette until the underside is golden brown.
5. Place the pan under a preheated grill until golden on the top.

Beetroot, Grain Mustard & Horseradish Relish

Preparation time: 5 mins

Ingredients
4 Medium Sized Cooked
Beetroots
4 tbls Grain Mustard
Handful of freshly grated
horseradish or tablespoon of
creamed horseradish

Method
1. Peel the beetroot, roughly
   chop and place in a food
   processor with the
   mustard and horseradish,
   blend to a paste and serve
   as a garnish to beef.

This relish will keep in a
sealed jar up to 3 days in the
refrigerator.

Bloomer's Bakewell Pork Pie

Ingredients
For the Pork Meat:
450g (1lb) Pork Meat
(shoulder) cut into small
chunks
A pinch of salt, white pepper
and sage

For the Water Crust:
450g (1lb) of strong white flour
224g ($^1/_2$ lb) of lard
Pinch of salt, white pepper
$^1/_4$ pint cold tap water

Method
1. Boil the water and lard
    together. Sieve flour, salt
    and pepper into a bowl.
    Make a well in the flour
    and pour in the hot water
    and lard. Mix together to
    form a paste.
    Cover and allow to cool.
2. Jelly or Stock.
    Boil two pigs' trotters for at
    least two hours. Add
    seasoning to taste. Cover
    and cool.
3. Place paste on a floured
    cold work surface. Save a
    quarter of the paste for the
    lid. Form the paste around
    a wooden pie mould (or a
    two pound jam jar).
4. Place meat into the hole
    that you have made and
    press down.
5. Roll out the rest of the
    pastry to form the lid.
    Moisten the lid with water.
    Place on top of your pie
    and crimp together with
    your fingers.

6. Make a small hole in the
    centre of the lid. Glaze
    with a beaten egg.
7. Place in a hot oven for 1$^1/_2$
    hours at 190/200˚C
8. Remove from the oven
    and stand for at least one
    hour.

9. Through the hole in the
    lid, fill the pork pie with the
    stock/jelly, until it comes
    to the top of the pie.
10. Cool and allow jelly to set.

The Bakewell Pork Pie

How things used to be.

Pork pies have been made at Bloomers bakehouse on
Buxton Road since 1820. Pigs were bought from
Bakewell market. They were then driven through the town
to the slaughter house/bake house where they were kept
in the hay loft, fed and watered and then slaughtered
when needed. They were then hung outside in the yard as
there were no fridges or chillers back then. They were
then used for the pork pies as required.

Cranberry Glazed Pork Roast

Preparation time: 15 mins
Cooking time: 30-45 mins
Oven temperature: 160˚C
Serves 6-8

Ingredients
2 kilo (4 lb) Pork Loin Roast
2 tsp Cornflour
$^1/_4$ tsp Cinnamon
Pinch of Salt
$^1/_2$ tbsp Grated Orange Peel
2 tbsp Orange Juice
1 Jar Whole Berry Cranberry
Sauce

Method
1. Over a medium heat place all the ingredients (except the pork) in a small saucepan and cook until thickened, set aside.
2. In a shallow baking dish place the roast and cook at 160˚C for 45 minutes. Spoon half of the glaze over the roast and continue to cook for a further 30 - 45 minutes.
3. Leave to stand for 10 minutes, slice and serve with the remaining sauce.

Chicken
Caesar Salad

Ingredients
4 Free Range Chicken Fillets, weighing
about 140g (5oz) each
2 tbsp Olive Oil
2 Cloves of Garlic, crushed

Croutons
3 Slices White Bread, Cubed
1 tbsp Olive Oil
25g (1oz) Butter
1 Cos Lettuce, washed
1 Clove of Garlic, crushed
4-6 tbsp of a good Caesar Salad
dressing, such as Mary Berry's

Garnish
Shaving of Parmesan Cheese

Method
Trim the chicken of any fat and place in a glass bowl with the
olive oil and crushed garlic to marinate, if time allows, for 1-2
hours.
Heat the Aga grill pan on the Simmering Plate, then transfer to
the boiling plate and heat for a further 2-3 minutes. Remove the
chicken fillets from the marinade and place them in the grill pan.
Cook for about 4-6 minutes until the chicken has been branded.
Turn the chicken over and transfer to the Roasting Oven.

2,3 and 4 Oven Aga: Place the grill pan on the floor of the
Roasting Oven and cook the chicken for a further 8-10 minutes
until done.

Conventional Cooking: Gradually heat the grill pan until hot and
cook the chicken on the hob

Rayburn: Gradually heat the grill pan on the hotplate, move over
to the hottest side. Add the chicken and cook one side. Turn
over and then transfer to the floor of a hot Main Oven to
complete cooking.

Whilst the chicken is cooking make the garlic croutons. Melt the
olive oil with the butter and garlic in an Aga cast aluminium
frying pan, add the cubes of bread and shake to coat with the
garlic mixture. Gently fry until golden, shaking frequently to
ensure even browning, either on the Simmering Plate or in the
oven. The handle of this pan is detachable so it is equally at
home on the hotplates or in the oven.
Break the lettuce leaves into bite size pieces and toss in an Aga
wooden bowl. Mix the Caesar dressing using the Aga salad
servers and place in the salad bowl. Serve with the warm sliced
chicken fillets.
Garnish with the croutons and shavings of parmesan.
Serves 4

Roast Chicken with Orange, Ginger & Honey

Ingredients

1 x 5lb (2.5kg) chicken
1 x 1 in piece of fresh ginger, finely chopped
1 x large orange, zest & juice
1 x tbs runny honey
salt & pepper
6 dried apricots, soaked and chopped small
2 slices bread, crumbed
1 x large onion or equivalent shallots, finely chopped
a little oil
2oz (50g) pine nuts

Gas 4, Elec 190c, Conv 180c

Method

1. Preheat the oven. Make the stuffing by sweating the chopped onion in a little oil until soft. Add 1 tsp of the chopped ginger, cook for a few minutes, then add the breadcrumbs and salt and pepper and stir over a faster heat until the crumbs begin to brown. (Add a little more oil if necessary).

2. Add enough stock and apricot soaking water to moisten the mixture, with a little orange zest, the apricots and pine nuts. Check and adjust seasoning. Stuff the chicken.

3. Loosen the skin of the chicken by pushing your fingers between the skin and the flesh. Mix the remaining orange zest and juice, honey and chopped ginger and spoon about 4tbs under the skin and spread evenly over breast legs. Pour the remainder over the outside of the bird. (If you do not eat the skin put all the mixture underneath). The honey will cause the skin to be quite dark and crisp when cooked.

4. Put the bird into a high-sided roasting dish to prevent fat spitting into the oven and roast for about 1½– 1¾ hrs, basting 2 or 3 times and turning around half way through cooking if necessary. Remove from the oven, cover with foil and a tea towel, and rest 15 minutes before carving.

A tasty pie can be made with any of the leftover chicken. Fry a little more onion and fresh ginger; add stock, orange juice and/or white wine. Add the chopped chicken and stuffing. Heat through and put in a pie dish. Top with pastry and bake Gas 5, Elec 210c, Conv 180c approx 25 minutes.

Warm Mustard and Saffron Salad with Smoked Salmon

Preparation time: 15 mins
Cooking time: 20 mins

Ingredients
450g (1lb) small new potatoes
Pinch of Saffron
Salt
1 Branch of Celery Leaves (reserving some to garnish)
110g (4oz) Smoked Salmon, diced

For the Sauce
1 tsp Mustard
$^1/_2$ tbls Vinegar
2 Pinches of Saffron
2 tbls Plain Yoghurt
Salt

Method
1. Peel the potatoes and place them in a large saucepan, cover with cold water, add salt, a pinch of saffron and the celery leaves. Bring to the boil and cook for 15 to 20 minutes.

2. Remove from heat and drain.
3. To make the sauce, place the yoghurt, mustard, vinegar, saffron and salt in a bowl and mix together.
4. Add the potatoes and the diced salmon to the sauce and gently toss to coat. Sprinkle with the chopped reserved celery leaves and serve.

Perfect Pasta and Cheese

Preparation time: 30 mins
Cooking time: 30 mins
Oven Temperature: 175°C

Ingredients
2 tsps margarine
$^1/_2$ cup minced shallots
2 cups sliced mushrooms
1$^1/_2$ cups sliced shiitake
mushroom caps (about 4oz)
$^1/_4$ tsps salt
$^1/_2$ tsps pepper
3 garlic cloves, minced
$^3/_4$ cup fresh breadcrumbs
2 cups (8oz) shredded
reduced-fat sharp cheddar
cheese, divided
$^1/_2$ cup chopped chives,
divided
3$^1/_2$ cups uncooked penne
(tubular-shaped pasta)

Method
1. Preheat oven to 175°C.
2. Prepare a Bechamel
   sauce and keep warm.
3. Melt margarine in a large
   nonstick pan over a
   medium-high heat.
4. Add shallots; sauté 1
   minute. Stir in
   mushrooms, salt, pepper,
   and garlic; sauté 3
   minutes or until liquid has
   evaporated. Set aside.
5. Combine breadcrumbs, $^1/_4$
   cup cheese, and 1
   tablespoon chives. Stir
   well; set aside.
6. Add 1$^3/_4$ cups cheese to
   the Bechamel sauce; stir
   until the cheese melts.

7. Cook the pasta according
   to package directions,
   omitting salt and oil. Drain
   well; return the pasta to
   the pan.
8. Add sauteed mushrooms,
   and shallots to the cheese
   sauce and 3 tablespoons
   of chives; stir well.
9. Spoon the pasta mixture
   into a 2 litre casserole;
   sprinkle with breadcrumbs
   mixture. Bake at 175°C for
   30 minutes.

Spiced Lamb Pittas with Quick Piccalilli

Preparation time: 15 mins

Ingredients
450g (1 lb) Lean Minced Lamb
2 tbsp Curry Paste
1 Garlic Clove
2 Gherkins, sliced
1 Cucumber, sliced
3 Cauliflower florets
$1/4$ Red Pepper, sliced
1 tbsp Vinegar (from Gherkin Jar)
2 tbsp Honey
1 tsp English Mustard

Method
1. Mix the gherkins, cucumber, cauliflower and red pepper. Add the vinegar, honey, mustard. Mix well and leave for the flavours to infuse.
2. Mix the lamb, curry paste and garlic. Shape into small patties and grill for 10 minutes or until cooked through.

Smoked Haddock Chowder
Smoked Haddock
and West Country Denhay Mature Cheddar

Preparation time: 20 mins
Cooking time: 30 mins

Ingredients
2 tbsp Olive Oil
40g (1¹/₂oz) Butter
2 Medium Onions, diced
1 Medium Leek, sliced
3 Celery Sticks, chopped
1 Glass of White Wine
350g (12oz) Potatoes, peeled and chopped
1 litre (1³/₄ pint)Vegetable Stock
570ml (1 pint) Milk
275ml (¹/₂ pint) Double Cream
500g (1lb 2oz) Natural Smoked Haddock, skinned and boneless
200g (7oz) Grated West Country Denhay Mature Cheddar
2 tbsp Parsley, chopped
Salt and Pepper
Extra Virgin Olive Oil

Method
1. Poach the haddock in the milk for 5-6 minutes, flake and leave in cooking liquor. Put to one side and allow to cool.
2. Melt the butter and oil and gently fry the onion, celery, leek and garlic for 5 minutes,
3. Add the white wine and reduce by half.
4. Add the potatoes., stock and season to taste, cook for 20 minutes.
5. Remove from the heat and add the haddock flakes and milk mixture.
6. Add half the cheese.
7. Serve into bowls and garnish with the remaining cheese, parsley and a drizzle of oil.

Roasted Beef with Pesto and Tomato, Herb Stuffing

Preparation time: 20 mins
Cooking time: Beef 20 mins per 450g (1 lb) plus 20 mins
Oven temperature: 175˚C

Ingredients
1130g (2¹/₂ lb) Lean Beef Joint
170g (6oz) Breadcrumbs
3 tbsp Red Pesto
1 tbsp Mixed Herbs, chopped
1 tsp Dried Mixed Herbs
2 Spring Onions, sliced
1 Tomato, chopped

Method
1. Place the beef in a roasting tin, cook in a preheated oven at 175˚C for specified time.
2. Mix the breadcrumbs, chopped tomato, spring onions, fresh herbs, dried herbs and 1 tbsp of red pesto.
3. Divide the mixture into 8 balls.
4. Remove the beef 20 minutes before it's cooked and coat with the red pesto. Place the stuffing balls around the joint, return to the oven and continue to cook.
5. Serve with vegetables. (Carrots with pine nuts, drizzled with honey makes a wonderful side dish.)

Roast Pork Tenderloin with Herb Potatoes

Preparation time: 5 mins
Cooking time: 40 mins
Oven temperature: 220°C

Ingredients
2 Pork Tenderloins
450g (1 lb) Small, White Potatoes
8 Bay Leaves
1/3 Cup Grapeseed Oil
4 tbsp Butter
2 Cups Veal Stock (or chicken stock)
Salt and Pepper

Method
1. Make 3 incisions in the potatoes, but do not cut all the way through. Spread some butter in each incision and sprinkle with salt. Place a bay leaf in the centre of each potato. Wrap in foil and place on a baking sheet.
2. Bake for 40 minutes at 220°C.
3. Heat the oil in a heavy bottomed frying pan, season the pork and sauté on both sides for about 10-15 minutes.

Remove from the heavy bottomed frying pan and place on a roasting pan, place in the oven and cook for about 15-20 minutes.
4. Pour the stock into the heavy bottomed frying pan and heat. Sieve the stock and return to the pan.
5. Bring to the boil, remove from the heat and add 1 tbsp butter in cubes and whisk in cube by cube.
6. Cut the pork into slices, place with the potatoes, pour over the sauce and serve.

Lamb Steak with ✗ Lemon and Chive Butter

Preparation time: 6 mins
Cooking time: 12 mins

Ingredients
4 Lean Lamb Steaks
25g (1oz) Butter
1 Lemon Zest
1 tsp Chives
$\frac{1}{2}$ tsp Black Peppercorns - crushed

Method
1. Cook the lamb steaks under the grill or BBQ for 8 - 12 minutes.
2. Mix the butter, lemon zest, chives and black peppercorns together.
3. Place a spoonful of the butter over the lamb and allow to melt slightly before serving, or form a circular pat using a small cutter and place on the lamb.
4. Serve with new potatoes and fresh green beans.

Khao Tom

Soothing rice, ginger and chicken soup

Preparation time: 5 mins
Cooking time: 25 mins
Serves 4

Ingredients:
2 tbsp groundnut oil
4 medium chicken breasts
80g (3oz) jasmine rice
1 litre clear chicken stock
2 tbsp fish sauce (nam pla)
1 tbsp light soy sauce
Freshly ground black pepper
40g (1½oz) very finely
chopped ginger

For the garnish
10 large garlic cloves peeled
and cut into 2mm slices
4 spring onions sliced
diagonally
3 medium red chillies sliced
thinly on the diagonal
Handful of freshly chopped
coriander

Method
1. Heat a wok until it is hot
   and starting to smoke
   slightly. Add the oil. Add
   the garlic and fry until it is
   a light brown colour.
2. Removed with a slotted
   spoon and pat dry with
   kitchen roll and place to
   one side.
3. Slice the chicken thinly
   and fry in the oil until
   sealed.
4. Drain the oil from the wok
   and add the chicken
   stock, soy sauce, fish
   sauce, chopped ginger
   and jasmine rice. Bring to
   the boil and allow to
   simmer gently for 12
   minutes or until the
   chicken and rice are
   cooked thoroughly.

5. Add the freshly ground
   black pepper.

Serve into four warmed soup
bowls and garnish with the
spring onion, chillies, fried
garlic and coriander.
Serve at once.

Fish and Chips

Preparation time: 25 mins
Cooking time: 15 mins

Ingredients (fish):
1 medium sized cod fillet per person
100g (4oz) plain flour
100g (4oz) self raising flour
5ml ($^1/_2$ tsp) salt
280ml ($^1/_2$ pt) milk and a splash of lager
15ml (1 tbsp) of oil
2 stiffly beaten egg whites
1 egg yolk
Water
You will also need:
Sunflower oil

Method:
1. Sift the flours and a pinch of salt into a basin. Make a well and add the egg yolk (keep the egg whites for the next step) and liquid and beat the mixture together until it's smooth. Leave the batter to rest for 30 minutes. You can add a little cold sparkling water to your rested batter to give it a lighter finish.
2. Meanwhile, whisk the egg whites until they are light and fluffy. Fold them into the rested batter mix and you are ready to go. If you like, you can use a splash of lager in your batter as it can give it a bit more flavour as well as more bubbles for a lighter covering.
3. Coat the fish lightly in seasoned flour. When ready, carefully hold the fish at the tail end and dip it into the batter. Use the side of a bowl to wipe the battered fish lightly to remove any excess.
4. The fat temperature in the fryer should be pre-heated to 180°C and the wire basket should be removed. Gently place the fish away from you into the oil to avoid splashes with the hot oil.
5. The fish should rise to the surface after 3-4 minutes and may need turning with a perforated spoon to ensure an even browning and crispy texture. After another 3-4 minutes the fish should be ready.

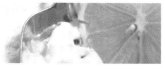

Ingredients (chips):
Allow 2 medium sized potatoes per person, preferably Maris Piper, washed and peeled sunflower oil.

Method:
1. Cut the potatoes into slices about 1cm ($^1/_2$in) thick, and 5cm (2ins) long. And then cut the slices into strips 5 x 1 x 1cm (2 x $^1/_2$ x$^1/_2$ins). Wash them well and dry them with a cloth.
2. Place them into the basket, and lower them carefully into the deep oil at 165°C. I find the best way to cook chips is by doing it in two stages so once the potato chip has softened and become "limp", drain it thoroughly trying not to shake the basket and damage the chips.
3. Put them aside on a plate.
4. When required for eating simply place the chips back into a basket. Increase the oil temperature to 180-185°C and lower the chips into the oil carefully. Cook them until they are crisp and golden then drain them well, season with salt and they're ready to eat.

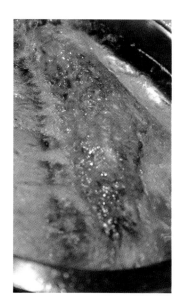

Duck Breast Fillets with Sour Cherries

Preparation time: 20 mins
Cooking time: 30 mins

Ingredients
2 Duck Breast Fillet
450g (1 lb) Sour Cherries
1 tbsp Aged Wine Vinegar
1 tbsp Blackcurrant Liqueur
3 tbsp Dry Red Wine
2 tsp Brown Sugar
1 Cup Chicken Stock
1 tbsp Unsalted Butter
Salt and Pepper

Method
1. Pit the cherries, reserving all the juice.
2. Season the duck on the skin side only. Heat a casserole dish over a medium heat and add the duck skin side down, cook for 20 minutes.
3. Remove the fat, turn the duck skin side up and cook for an additional 5 minutes, pricking the skin to allow more fat to run out.
4. Remove the duck from the casserole dish and place on a warmed plate, cover to keep warm.
5. Discard all the fat, return the casserole to the heat and add the vinegar, cook until it partly evaporates.
6. Add the liqueur, wine, sugar and the cherries with the juice. Boil for 1 minute. Drain the cherries over a bowl to reserve the liquid. Transfer the cherries to a dish and return the cooking liquid to the casserole.
7. Add the chicken stock and reduce the cooking juices until you have $1/4$ cup of liquid left. Pour in the juices from the rested duck breasts and any cherry juice, reduce until syrupy.
8. Remove from heat and whisk in the butter.
9. Slice the duck thinly on a plate, mound the cherries over some of the duck, coat with the sauce and serve.

...and then
to **finish.**

Baked Apple Stuffed with Wild Thyme and Herb Honey

Preparation time: 15 mins
Cooking time: 50 mins
Oven temperature: 200°C

Ingredients
4 Bramley Apples
50g (2oz) Ground Almonds
50g (2oz) Sultanas
3 tbsp Wild Thyme and Fragrant Herb Honey
25g (1oz) Butter

Topping
1 Small tub Greek Yoghurt
2 tbsp Wild Thyme and Fragrant Herb Honey
Sprigs of Fresh Thyme

Method
1. Preheat the oven to 200°C.
2. Core the apples and score the skins.
3. Mix the almonds, sultanas, wild thyme and herb honey in a bowl.
4. Fill the centre of each apple with the mixture and place a knob of butter over the top.
5. Grease an ovenproof dish and, with a spatula lift the apples into the dish. Spoon over 4 tablespoons of water around the base and bake for 45-50 minutes, until the apples are tender.
6. Stir some of the thyme and herb honey into the yoghurt.
7. Serve in a bowl with a spoonful of the yoghurt and decorate with small sprigs of fresh thyme.

Charlotte's Goo

Preparation time: 25 mins

Ingredients
8 Triffle Sponges
200g Jam
200g Amaretti Biscuits
750g Morello Cherries
Juice of 1/2 Lemon
250ml Sherry
750g Mascarpone Cheese
100g Sugar
2 eggs, separated
Toasted Flaked Almonds to
sprinkle on top

Method
1. Slice the Triffle Sponges in half, spread each sponge with half the jam and wedge them all in the bottom of a glass triffle dish.
2. Crush 150g of the amaretti biscuits over the triffle sponges and pour 150ml of the sherry over the top.
3. In a saucepan put the remaining jam, juice of half a lemon and melt for 2 minutes over a low heat. Add the cherries and stir until the juices start to run. Pour over the triffle biscuits.
4. Whisk the 2 egg yolks and caster sugar together, until a pale yellow colour, drizzle in 50ml of sherry whilst whisking.
5. In another bowl, whisk the 2 egg whites until soft peaks, stir into the mascarpone cheese. Add the remaining sherry and mix.
6. Mix the mascarpone cheese mixture together with the sugar and egg yolks.
7. Pour the mixture over the the cherries.
8. Sprinkle the toasted flaked almonds together with the remaining crushed amaretti biscuits over the top of the triffle.

Cheese Scones

Preparation time: 15 mins
Cooking time: 15 mins
Oven temperature: 230°C

Ingredients
225 gram (8oz) Plain Flour
$^1/_2$ Tsp Salt
Cayenne Pepper
2 $^1/_2$ Tsp Baking Powder
56g (2oz) Butter
112g (4oz) Grated Cheese
150ml ($^1/_4$ Pint) Milk
Beaten Egg or Milk to Glaze

Method
1. Sieve the flour, salt, baking powder and cayenne pepper into a bowl. Rub in the butter until the mixture resembles fine breadcrumbs
2. Add the grated cheese, and enough milk to give a soft dough.
3. Kneed lightly and roll out to $^3/_4$ inch thickness. Cut into 2 inch rounds, brush tops with the beaten egg or milk and bake for 12-15 minutes at 230°C.
4. Halve and spread with butter.

Damson Ice Cream

Ingredients
450g (1 lb) Damsons
113g (4oz) Soft Brown Sugar
$^1/_2$ Pint Water
4 Free Range Egg Yolks
113g (4oz) Icing Sugar
$^1/_2$ Pint Double Cream
2 tbsp Iced Water
Chocolate coated ginger,
sliced to decorate

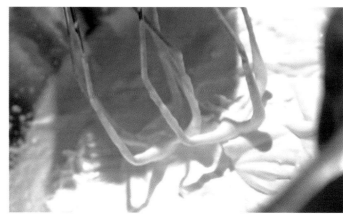

Method
1. In a saucepan place the damsons, sugar and water bring to the boil, cover and simmer for 10 minutes until the fruit is tender.
2. Press the fruit through a sieve, and chill in the fridge.
3. Place a bowl over some simmering water, and beat the egg yolks with the icing sugar until warm.
4. Take off the heat and continue to beat until the mixture has trebled in size, then chill in the fridge.
5. Whisk the cream and iced water to soft peaks.
6. Whisk the damson puree, egg mixture and cream lightly together, freeze until partially frozen.
7. Vigorously whisk the ice cream once partially frozen then re-freeze.
8. Serve in glass dishes and decorate with sliced chocolate coated ginger.

Chocolate and Almond Battenburg Cake

Preparation time: 40 mins
Cooking time: 30-40 mins
Oven temperature: 170°C

Ingredients
225g (8oz) Almond Paste
110g (4oz) Butter, softened
110g (4oz) Caster Sugar
110g (4oz) Self Raising Flour
50g (2oz) Ground Rice
2 Eggs, lightly beaten
3-4 tbsp Apricot Jam
1/2 tsp Baking Powder
Almond Essence
Chocolate Powder (Cocoa)

Pre-heat oven to 170°C: Gas 3

1. Grease and line a large oblong baking tin with buttered greaseproof paper.
    Whisk together the butter and sugar until light and creamy. Add the beaten eggs gradually with a little of the flour. Fold in the remaining sieved flour, ground rice, baking powder and a few drops of almond essence.
2. Spoon half the mixture into one half of the prepared baking tin. Use a strip of buttered greaseproof paper to create a barrier.
3. Add a large tablespoon of chocolate powder (Cocoa) to the remaining mixture to turn it a dark brown colour.

Spoon into the other half of the tin, smoothing the surface.

4. Bake for 35-40 minutes or until well risen and springy to the touch and has shrunk slightly in the tin. Turn out and cool on a wire rack. When cool, trim the edges and cut lengthwise into four equal parts.
5. Place the jam into a saucepan and heat gently to melt. Brush the portions

of cake with the jam to stick them together to form a chequer-board effect.

6. Roll out the almond paste into a rectangle, long enough to wrap around the cake. Brush the outside of the cake with jam. Press the almond paste around the cake, dampening the edges lightly to form a neat join at one of the corners of the cake.
7. Trim the ends to neaten and decorate as wished.

Bread and Butter Pudding

Preparation time: 10 mins
Cooking time: 1 hour
Oven temperature: 170°C

Ingredients
7 Slices bread (crusts removed)
Soft Butter
1lt (1³/₄ pints) Milk
110g (4oz) Sugar
110 (4oz) Raisins and sultanas
3 eggs, slightly beaten
1 tsp Vanilla
¹/₂ tsp Cinnamon
¹/₄ tsp Salt

Method:
1. Pre-heat oven to 170°C: 325°F: gas 3.
2. Butter a large ovenproof baking dish.
3. Spread the butter generously on one side of each slice of bread.
4. Line bottom and sides of the dish with buttered bread.
5. Mix the milk, eggs, sugar, raisins and sultanas, vanilla, cinnamon and salt and pour over the bread.
5. Place a few extra pieces of buttered bread on top, press down to submerge.
7. Allow to stand for at least 30 minutes.
8. Cover, place in a bain-marie and bake for 30 minutes. Remove the lid and cook for a further 30 minutes until top becomes deep golden.

Pickled Pears

Preparation time: 30 mins

Ingredients
2 kilo (4lb) Pears
2 sticks of Cinnamon
Rind of 1 Lemon
450g (1 lbs) Soft light brown
sugar
1 tbsp Cloves
570ml (1 Pint) Cider Vinegar

Method
1. Pour the vinegar and
   sugar into a large
   saucepan and heat until
   the sugar has dissolved.

2. Peel, halve and core the
   pears and place in the
   saucepan along with the
   lemon rind and spices,
   simmer for about 10
   minutes until the pears
   are soft.
3. Remove the pears and
   place in a preserving jar.
4. Continue to boil the liquid
   until syrupy.
5. Pour the liquid over the
   pears and seal the jar.

This pickle will last for up to
six months in the fridge.
Serve with cold meats or
cheese.

Citrus Poppy Seed Cake

Preparation time: 30 mins
Cooking time: 50 mins
Oven temperature: 130°C

Ingredients
170g (6oz) Butter
170g (6oz) Caster Sugar
3 Eggs, Beaten
250g (9oz) Self Raising Flour
57g (2oz) Poppy Seeds
Grated Rind of 2 Oranges
Grated Rind of 2 Lemons
4tbsp Natural Yogurt

Topping
250g (9oz) Mascarpone
Grated rind and juice of 1
small Orange
3tbsp Orange or Lemon Curd
Grated rind of 1 Lemon

Method
1   Butter and line the base of
    a deep 20cm (8ins) cake
    tin.
2   Using a wooden spoon,
    or electric blender,
    beat together the butter,
    sugar, eggs, flour, poppy
    seeds, citrus rinds and
    yogurt until smooth.

3   Spread the mixture in a tin
    and bake at 130°C for 45-
    50 minutes until just firm.
    Cool in the tin for 10
    minutes, turn out onto a
    wire rack.
4   To make the topping mix
    the mascarpone with
    enough orange juice to
    make a spreadable icing.
    Swirl in the curd to give a
    marble effect. Spread
    over the cake and scatter
    with the grated rind.

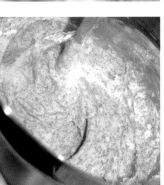

Shortbread

Preparation time: 10 mins
Cooking time: 40 mins
Oven temperature: 180°C

Ingredients
225g (8oz) Butter
110g (4oz) Icing Sugar
110g (4oz) Cornflour
Pinch of Salt

Method
1. Cream the butter and sugar thoroughly until soft and light.
2. Gradually work in the flour, add a pinch of salt and kneed until smooth.
3. Press into a 12 inch tin and bake for 35-40 minutes at 180°C.
4. Dredge with caster sugar while still hot and leave in the tin until cold.

For a variation dip the shortbread fingers into melted chocolate, place on baking parchment and chill until set.

Blackberry Whip

Preparation time: 15 mins
Plus 40 mins chilling time
Serves 4

Ingredients
2 Egg Whites
Pinch of Salt
$^1/_4$ cup Sugar
Grated rind of one lemon
1 tbsp Lemon Juice
1 pint Blackberries

Method
1. Beat the egg whites with
    salt until stiff. Beat in the
    sugar gradually. Beat until
    thick and glossy.
2. Fold in the lemon rind,
    juice and blackberries.
3. Chill.
4. Serve either on its own or
    with custard.

Chocolate Cheese Cake

Preparation time: 30mins
Cooking time: 60 mins
Oven temperature: 160°C

Ingredients
225g (8oz) Plain chocolate
digestive biscuits
85g (3oz) Butter
Filling:
700g (1lb 9oz) Cream cheese
175g (6oz) Caster sugar
3 tablespoons plain flour
2 teaspoons Vanilla essence
3 Eggs
112g (4oz) Plain chocolate,
broken
56g (2oz) Milk chocolate,
broken
56g (2oz) White chocolate

Method:

1. Line and grease the base of a 9 inch spring form tin with foil.
2. Crush biscuits into crumbs. Melt butter in a saucepan then stir in biscuit crumbs.
3. Press around the base of tin and cool in the refrigerator for 1 hour.
4. Preheat the oven to 160°C/325F/ gas mark 3.
5. Beat the cream cheese in a bowl until fluffy, add sugar, flour and vanilla essence, beat until smooth. Gradually beat in the eggs.
6. Separate half the mixture into another bowl. Melt the plain and milk chocolate in separate bowls over a pan of simmering water, leave to cool.
7. Stir the plain chocolate and milk into one of the cream cheese mixtures and the white chocolate into the other.
8. Pour the 2 mixtures alternately over the biscuit base, then using a knife swirl the mixtures to create a marbled effect.
9. Bake for 50-60 minutes. Leave in the oven with the door ajar until cold, then refrigerate for 2 hours before removing the chocolate cheesecake from the tin.

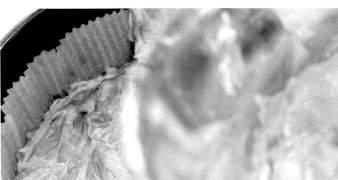

Very Berry Scone

Preparation time: 20 mins
Cooking time: 80 mins
Oven temperature: 170˚C

Ingredients
375g (13oz) Demerara Sugar
1kg (2lb 4oz) Self Raising Flour
4 Eggs – med
250g (9oz) Margarine
1kg (2lb 4oz) Frozen fruit mix
25ml (1floz) Milk

This recipe uses a 10 inch round flan dish and can serve up to 12 (depending on your hunger!)

Method

1. Pre heat oven to 170˚C
2. Defrost fruit mixture and leave to drain juice away.
3. In a mixer combine the flour, sugar, 3 eggs and margarine until mixed into a firmish dough. Remove from mixer and cut into 2 halves.
4. Lightly flour your surface and roll first half to approximately 1.5 cm thickness, this should be enough to cover the base of the dish.
5. Empty the fruit mixture into lined base (try to make sure that the juice has gone)
6. Brush the edges of the 1st half with milk (this will enable the top half to seal. Roll 2nd half of scone mixture to the same thickness and place over the top of the dish and push edge to seal.
7. With the final egg, whisk and brush the top of the very berry scone. Sprinkle with Demerara sugar.
8. Place in middle of oven for 40mins. Then turn oven down to 150˚C and bake for a further 40 mins. Remove when lightly golden - Enjoy !

In the summer you can use any fresh soft fruit you want.

The Manager
of Bourne's Restaurant,
Barry Garton has selected this
delicious and very popular
choice from his current menu.

In the courtyard at Denby Visitor Centre is Bourne's Restaurant.

Open during the day for snacks, lunches and afternoon teas, Bourne's has a distinctively contemporary interior that blends well with the traditional atmosphere of the visitor centre. As you step through the door be prepared to be tempted by a delicious selection of freshly baked cakes, along with the aroma of ground coffee! The lunch menu always has a Derbyshire dish of the day, salad selections and healthy choices for kids. Bourne's was refurbished last year, and now has a choice of seating areas including a summer roof terrace and the Danesby Room - or you can simply sit outside on a bench in the cobbled courtyard.

Bourne's is open daily 9.30 - 4.30pm.

The Cookery Emporium at Denby Visitor Centre sells everything for the discerning cook, as well as locally produced foods. Denby Visitor Centre also reguarly holds local Food Fayres including a very popular Christmas Food and Gift Fayre - see www.denbyvisitorcentre.co.uk for details.

Irish Coffee

Preparation time: 10 mins

Ingredients
3-4 cl (or 3 glugs!) Whiskey
1 tsp Brown Sugar
Freshly brewed strong Coffee
2-3 tbsp double Cream

Method
1. Warm a stemmed glass with hot water and dry off.
2. Pour the whiskey in the glass and the sugar, stir until dissolved.
3. Pour in the coffee. Leave a gap of about 1cm from the top of the glass.
4. Pour the cream onto the coffee over the back of a teaspoon to stop the cream from splitting.

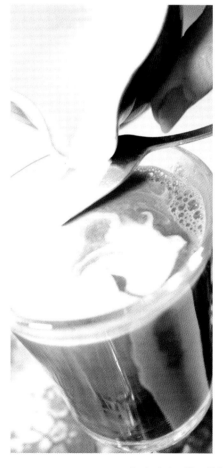

Cheese Board

Traditionally the serving of cheese is usually at the end of the meal. But cheese can easily be served as a dessert, and many people particularly the Italians and the French like to finish sipping their wine with their cheese. The perfect cheeseboard usually consists of three or four perfectly selected cheeses, invariably offering a contrast of flavours and textures. Here in Derbyshire we are proud of our two signature cheeses, Stilton and Sage Derby. Blue Stilton is a rich creamy and tangy tasting cheese often eaten with biscuits and accompanied by a quality Port, whereas Sage Derby is one of those cheeses which can be appreciated more with a good robust red Claret.

Two other cheeses which enhance the cheeseboard are Brie (try the exquisite Cornish Brie available from good quality cheese shops) but if you prefer a traditional full textured mature Cheddar, then West Country farmhouse cheddar is the ideal partner for the cheeseboard.

But what do you eat with the cheese? Fruit is the classic combination that provides a balanced dessert that requires little preparation and is not too sweet. Try fresh pears or hazelnuts with the Brie, dried figs and walnuts with the Stilton and crisp apples such as Cox's with our beloved Sage Derby.

If you are ever in doubt about which fruit or biscuit should accompany your choice of cheese, ask your local cheese purveyor.

Companies creating the **perfect environment**

Food looks
so much better on
fine tableware

Tastes and fashions may change but the decorative and artistic skills that make our wares stand out are as popular today as they have ever been. Renowned for 250 years for the manufacture of lightly potted and exquisitely decorated porcelain and bone china, Royal Crown Derby is synonymous with superlative quality and distinctive productions - including tableware, giftware and the paperweights and miniatures that are highly collectable today.

Royal Crown Derby

To view the range call at our showroom on Osmaston Road, Derby or visit our web site www.royalcrownderby.co.uk

Find out why our kitchens stand out from the rest!

Serious Cookers for Serious Cooks

™

Your Local LACANCHE Range Cooker Service Engineer • Installation • Service • Repairs •
All work carried out by trade recognised and fully qualified experienced service & LPG specialist engineers.

Companies to
provide the
ingredients

The ingredients

fruit&vegwholesale

Telephone: *3am-10am* 01332 363663 or 01332 380612
Mobile: 07968 736159   Fax: 01332 382383
Email: info@mandbfruits.co.uk

Large Enough to Cope
Small Enough to Care

A valued customer with
an array of our produce

A small business established for around 30 years offering a caring, reliable service
to all its customers. M & B Fruits has evolved from providing fresh produce to small
retail shops into a highly efficient business, providing produce, exotic fruit and vegetables
to a large cosmopolitan market including restaurants, hotels, golf clubs,
retail shops, public and private schools etc...

We operate 6 days a week, delivering within a twenty mile radius of Derby
and make every effort to deliver in the morning.

If you are interested in our service, or think we may be able to assist your business or
require more information, please contact M & B Fruits by either Telephone, Fax or e-mail.

Oakfield Farm Shop

Oakfield Farm, Belper Road,
Stanley Common
www.oakfieldfarm.co.uk
Telephone: 0115 930 5358

*'Where we are
what you eat'*

Suppliers of fresh fruit and vegetables.
Free-range eggs (GM free). Home produced
Hereford beef. Lamb, turkeys, chickens.
Home made sausage and burgers
Locally sourced pork

delivering quality

12 December 2006

Dear Paul

It's been about a year now since our association with you began and we are so pleased with the way things are going, we just had to put pen to paper.

Since you have been butchering our beef, our sales have almost trebled. The presentation and traceability of the meat makes all the difference. The steaks and joints are cut perfectly into meal-sized portions and the packing and labelling give it all the professional touch.

Your obliging, helpful and "can do" attitude is much appreciated and we can always rely on you to make sure our beef is hung for the perfect amount of time.

Once the animal has left our hands it's nice to be able to relax and be confident that you and the guys at Mainstream will take care of all the rest.

When we first met, you took the time to show us around, and made us feel special and we were very impressed with what we saw.

Our customers are telling us how important it is to them that their meat is home-reared, hung and packed nicely and without your expertise our business would not be thriving the way it is, in fact right now, we have more customers than meat!

We are looking forward to striding into the New Year and hope our association with Mainstream is a long and happy one.

Kind regards

Dave Hunt & Sarah Bexon
Manor Farm Fold, Chesterfield Road, Oakerthorpe
ALFRETON Derbyshire
DE55 7LP

*M*ainstream
International Foods

Stonebroom Industrial Estate
Stonebroom
Alfreton
Derbyshire DE55 6LQ

Telephone: 01773 591177
Fax: 01773 591178
www.mainstreamfoods.co.uk

St Clement's Bakery

Bolsover, Chesterfield.
Telephone 01246 822655
Fax 01246 826222

Bakers of fine quality speciality
breads, cakes, pies and sweets.

Vegetarian Pies, Steak and Guinness Pies,
Steak and Potato Pies, Chicken and Mushroom,
Roast Mediterranean Vegetable Pies etc.
Traditional Cakes, Ginger Bread, Bakewell Tarts
and Parkin.

All available at your local farmers markets
including Bakewell, Chesterfield & Buxton.

Speciality orders by request.

and now
the **inspiration**

Melbourne Arms
Cuisine India
for the best of Indian Cuisine

The restaurant for Indian cuisine, provided by experienced purveyors of fusion cooking for some forty years.
Mr Darshan Kumar and his wife Shanti are ably assisted by their staff, recruited from some of the best hotels in the sub continent of India.

Mr Kumar was always going to be in the restaurant business. From the very early days of his education and later during his time at university in India, his interest was always in cooking and the different dishes available in the DHABAS (Roadside eateries).Indeed his early attempts at replicating these dishes form the very contemporary menu the Melbourne Arms Restaurant now offers its clients.

After coming to the UK, shortly after his marriage to Shanti, herself an exceptional cook, they commenced their search for premises to start their own restaurant. Initially they tried to do this in Scotland (Aberdeen), but with no success and so they moved to Derbyshire. In the city of Derby they achieved their aim and set up a small restaurant in Normanton Road.

The Full Moon as it was named, soon blossomed from its small beginnings to the restaurant of choice, for up to 200 sit down diners every night. It also did a brisk trade in delivered "take away" meals.All this was achieved at the same time as their young family was growing up. Both sons were given a good grounding in the business.

Family imperatives in the end made it necessary to expand the operation. Mr Kumar's elder son elected to move to Oxford and set up his own restaurant businesses.The Melbourne Arms was purchased for the "younger" son "Nes" who played "mine host" for several years, successfully establishing it as the premier Indian Restaurant in the area.

Family problems some 5-6 years ago made it necessary for Mr Kumar to come out of retirement, and take on the full time management of the business.This he did with his

usual vigour, bringing all his not inconsiderable knowledge to the enterprise, not to mention many of his oldest clients from the Full Moon Tandoori.

The Melbourne Arms is today a modern restaurant in Melbourne. It has a fully air conditioned dining area, which can cater for 100 diners. It can also provide full bed and breakfast accommodation for up to 14 people in smart en suite rooms.There is also car parking for 50 cars in its off street car park, fully monitored by CCTV cameras.The grounds encompass nicely grassed areas with outdoor seating properly fenced, and some recreational facilities for children to play in safety (weather permitting).

A minibus with capacity for 16 persons is available for clients to book.This is free for parties of eight or more, covering a radius of 6 miles.

The carefully chosen menu, which caters for all the old favourites, like Chicken Tikka Masala, Rogan Josh, Bhuna, Dupiaza,Vindaloo etc, has lately been considerably extended to provide some delectable additions, in some instances unique to the Melbourne Arms.They include such items as Murgh Kali Mirch (Chicken with Black Pepper), Marriage of Convenience (Chicken mixed with fish) and Chicken Samarkand and many others.

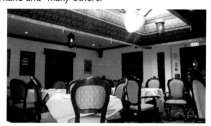

The menu also caters for the calorie conscious clients with the special "Lean Cuisine" section, providing low fat dishes for the health conscious diners.Also available is the "English Menu" and of course a children's menu.

On Sundays there is the very popular buffet "Eat as much as you like for a set price". They provide a selection of some 25 dishes, both starters and main dishes, and of course the accompanying poppadums, pickles and naan breads.This is particularly good value for money for all the family.

Pay them a visit and give it a try!

92, Ashby Road, Melbourne. 01332 864949

Masa Restaurant and Wine Bar

The old Wesleyan chapel which for the last three years has een home to this excellent restaurant, stands proudly back rom the road on an apron of green lawn on Brook Street in Derby. The owners have lovingly converted the chapel into n airy and spacious restaurant, whilst still sympathetically etaining many of its fine feature which are part of its distinctive character. The simple contemporary decor complements the bold strong lines of the original building.

We dined at Masa on a mild Spring evening, and on entering we found plenty of comfortable sofas and chairs arranged around a central bar over which the original pulpit stood. The quiet and competent staff soon made us welcome, and while we enjoyed pre dinner drinks we chose from a very imaginative menu. There is plenty of space here for larger party groups which makes it ideal for anyone celebrating a special occasion, but if you just want an intimate evening for two, you don't feel hemmed in by others. After ordering a bottle of Pinot Noir, (priced around £25), we were shown up the stairs to where the tables are arranged around the original balcony, and seated by one of the original front windows where we watched the light fade over the town.

Masa offer a three course set diner menu (£21 Monday to Friday) with two choices for each course, or you can have a free choice. While we waited we were served with a selection of warm speciality breads and oil and balsamic to dip into. To begin I had filo wrapped petit crottin, which is a type of goats cheese, it was wrapped in fine flaky filo, and was warm crumbly and creamy inside with four wafer thin beetroot squares and a lovely balsamic and oil dressing. My companions broccoli soup was fresh, thick and hot, a very pleasant start to his meal.

Slow roasted blade of beef followed, and as I put my fork into the meat it just fell apart, with a reduced balsamic glaze the flavour was intense, rich and extremely tender. Although

it sat on a bed of savoy cabbage, with a rosette of sliced potatoes, we also were served with a dish of seasonal vegetables. My companions John Dory sat on a bed of wilted spinach, a firm white fish with a mild flavour.

Our desserts were to die for, decorated with the finest of crisp ginger biscuit and a foaming sauce my lightly caramelised lime torte was absolutely exquisite, and my companions open pastry tartlet filled with almond looked really tempting.

As each course arrived we were delighted by its beautiful presentation. The flavours were controlled, sometimes intense, sometimes subtle, some sweet, some sharp, but each time in keeping with the balance of the whole dish. The tables were decorated with a single lily, and our glasses were kept constantly filled with either wine or water. This is a beautiful place to dine, where the experience of the chef shines through.

The Old Wesleyan Chapel, Brook Street, Derby
01332 203345

Dining out at
BLENHEIM

Entering Blenheim House in Etwall for the first time one winter evening, I was struck by its own individual character, and without even speaking with Peter the owner, its slightly French, Provencal influence underscored the atmosphere.

Rustic stone and red tile floors with original stoves and fireplaces and many of the houses other features mixed with contemporary comfortable seating, to create a very relaxed and pleasant ambiance. The bar seems to be the hub of activity for both the hotel and for dining, and after introducing ourselves we found a quiet corner to ponder the menu over a 'G and T'.

The menu is huge, that is in physical size, and includes informative notes about local produce used, almost everything they serve is produced in their own kitchens.

Here they have a dedication to supporting local producers, which for the diner means that ingredients haven't been flown half way around the world before they land on your plate, also they are a little more unusual and add a variety.

Home made bread and a dish of green olive oil with balsamic vinegar was on our table to dip into while we waited for our starter. My companion chose risotto to begin, with roasted red peppers, and rocket salad, it was creamy but not sticky, with large shavings of parmesan, "delicious" he said. I was tempted by the roasted fresh figs with smooth goat's cheese and rocket, the fresh flavour of the figs complementing the creamy cheese, and peppery taste of rocket. It was really lovely.

The beef tempted my companion as usual, and I must say his rolled rib-eye steak looked very appetizing, served with a stack of chunky chips and a side salad. It is quite some time however, since I enjoyed trout but mine was a pale fillet with a gentle flavour, nicely moist and with a few flaked almonds, green beans and a light creamy sauce it was a simple traditional dish, well cooked. A bowl of mixed seasonal

HOUSE

vegetables accompanied our meal, and we shared a side order of rocket salad with finely sliced onions, a generous amount of goats cheese and baby tomatoes.

The food here at Blenheim House is ample but not over-powering, a well balanced and designed menu, and as we took our leisure, we had room for their beautifully presented desserts. My companions milk chocolate cheese cake was delicious, a crunchy base with a topping not too sweet. My lemon dessert was the perfect finish, tangy and rich with buttery home-made short cake to accompany it. We finished with fresh coffee.

It is always a pleasure to find somewhere new to dine, and we really enjoyed our evening. Peter's training with a two Michelin starred chef in France, and alongside top chefs in London, has well equipped him to produce excellent food, in relaxed and friendly surroundings. Head chef Richard Strydom, has certainly created a superb menu. We thoroughly enjoyed a fantastic meal. At present Blenheim House is set on a schedule of steady refurbishment both inside and out, it will be something to look forward to with relish.

To book call 01283 732254

Dining out at the bay tree

Just our third visit to Melbourne and I am already enchanted by the small red brick market town. An array of pretty shops surround the market place where we found our dining venue for this evening, the bay tree Restaurant. The soft lighting looked welcoming and as we entered, we were greeted by Vicki, one of the partners who have owned and run the restaurant for the last 18 years. The décor is contemporary but inviting and warm and, as we were shown past the seating area to our table I noted the intimate atmosphere.

We were brought a bowl of large shiny black & green olives to nibble on as we indulged in a G and T and read through the menu. Starting with the main course I chose to order the seared salmon served with sweet citrus asparagus and dill hollandaise although the fresh halibut steak presented with a roast beetroot and balsamic compote and a sauce vierge looked very tempting. My partner, true to form, selected the roasted fillet of prime English beef 'Rossini' - bay tree style. Now from here we worked back to the starters and it was a difficult choice, but eventually I chose Parma ham, very thinly sliced and not in the least stringy, topped with a mixed leaf salad dressed in the subtlest of dressings, a circle of warm, creamy goat's cheese on a small crouton of bread completed this delightful starter. A quick dip into my companions Jerusalem globe artichoke and carrot soup revealed it to have a slightly spicy kick to it. As he tipped the bowl to extract the last drops, I didn't have to ask if he enjoyed it.

I noticed the miniature silver domed server over the butter, just one of the nice finishing touches which showed

the attention to detail here at the bay tree.

After a suitable pause, our main course arrived. Waxing lyrically about his steak, my companion sliced into it, to reveal the succulent pink centre - "now that's how the perfect steak should be cooked" he said. Sitting on top of a potato rosti and topped with a foie gras and duck liver pate, it really did look excellent and - with a small dish of seasonal vegetables and a red wine jus - not too rich, not too intense, very slightly fruity, in fact just right!

My salmon was delightful also, with a roasted tomato complementing the sweet flavour of the salmon, the acute crispness of the asparagus spears, and the not overpowering dill hollandaise, embellished with finely chopped chives. The warm potato salad was just enough to complete the experience.

The dessert menu was not to disappoint, and when our creations arrived, it seemed a shame to eat them as they were so beautifully and artistically presented. The fresh strawberries sharpened by the balsamic vinegar balanced with a muscatel dessert wine, layered with freshly made shortcake

rounds topped with crème fraiche on a plate decorated with drizzled chocolate. My liquorice parfait with Armagnac prunes and a lime and pernod jelly were exquisite, with butterfly wings of spun sugar, this was such a sophisticated take on a childhood favourite.

Finishing with the smoothest of coffees we were delighted to meet the other two partners, chef Rex and his wife Suzy, who created the desserts. We had thoroughly enjoyed our evening, and in retrospect, I can appreciate the difference that 13 years of flair makes to a dining experience. They have listened to their customers, ironed out all the glitches, sourced all the best ingredients, made you smile as you read the menu and the result - is a 'well oiled' (excuse the pun) extremely professional restaurant, a delight to visit, and one to be recommended without reservation.

Potter Street, Melbourne. 01332 863358

A Real Taste of the Orient

Siam Corner

Thai Village Restaurant and Bar.

The friendly smiles said it all, welcome to the Thai Village restaurant. Cheerful smiling faces set the tone for what was to become a most enjoyable evening.

As a lover of Thai food, my expectations were high; having dined at various Thai restaurants across Yorkshire and Derbyshire my partner and I were looking forward to seeing if the menus would differ from the other establishments we had frequented. Dining early was a bonus, we had the full attention of the waitresses, each one determined to give an excellent service, and always with a smile.

Choosing our meal from a selection of set menus was a perfect way to sample the huge array of dishes which Thailand is famous for. The Khantoke Seafood Set 6 course meal at on £25.00 per person started with Ta-Lay Tord, a dish of mixe sea food cooked in a crispy batter and served with plur sauce, this Moorish starter titillated the taste buds.

Many of the ingredients used in Thai cookery are no readily available from your local Asian Supermarkets and hav now become common place in our daily cooking , e.g. lemo grass, coconut milk, Kaffir lime leaves, and the sticky Thai ric which accompanied the main courses. Even though we ca buy these exotic ingredients and attempt to recreate Tha cuisine, the cooks and chefs at Thai Village have that extr ability to turn basic ingredients into a mouth-waterin banquet.

After enjoying our Po Tak, a soup made with tiger prawns mussels and squid, with overtones of lemon grass and basil, we were delighted with the excellent Pla Murk Satay, a persona

favourite of mine. The charcoal grilled squid marinated in Thai spices and tamarind sauce creates a glowing sensation in the cheeks and its long lasting taste is a pleasure.

Three courses down and three to go! After a slight interlude to benefit our digestive system we were up and running with the main course, Goong Pud Bai HoRa Par. This clean tasting dish of prawns, basil, onions, and red and green peppers was superb, by combining these ingredients with a little bit of Thai know how the Thai Village and its chefs recreate all that is good in their cookery. Goong Pud Bai HoRa Par was followed by Choo Chee Ta-Lay, Yam Sam Grab, Mee Grob, the Thai Dessert of the Day and Jasmine Tea.

The idea of a six course banquet may be too much for you, so choosing from the a la carte menu maybe the answer. Whilst sea food plays a major part in the Thai Villages menu,

dishes of chicken, roast duck, and beef are always available, there are over fifteen specialist vegetarian dishes to choose from, and if you must, you can even have a bowl of chips.

No visit to a Thai restaurant can be made without reference to the artistic array of sculptured vegetables, the skill and dexterity of the chefs was amazing, many of their creations should have a frame around them and be hung on the walls.

Much time and deliberation has gone into the decor of the restaurant, recreating the oriental feel that many tourists experience whilst visiting Thailand. The public of Chesterfield and Derby are lucky, they don't need to fly thousands of miles to experience real Thai food, and if the idea of fresh tasting, aromatic and exotic food appeals to you, then I urge you to visit Siam Corner Thai Village restaurant and bar.

The inspiration

Neil and Sue welcome all to

THE OLD SMITHY

Licensed Cafe & Village Shop

Chapel Hill, Beeley DE4 2NR
Telephone 01629 734666

Daily Menus
All our food is home made

'It's delicious'

Your local supplier of bread, cakes, pies, butter, cream,
milk, fruit, vegetables, oils, herbs, chocolates,
daily newspapers plus much, much more.

PART OF THE ST CLEMENTS BAKERY GROUP

Buckingham's

*The Restaurant with
one table and a hotel*

Newbold Road Chesterfield
Derbyshire S41 7PU

Be the first to taste this unique
dining experience

Where excellence
comes as standard

- Minimum booking 2 persons
- Restaurant reservation available. Phone for details
- Due to popular demand, Buckingham's is now open for lunch
- Cookery courses: enjoy a day in a professional kitchen with
  Master Chef Nick Buckingham
- Accommodation available in our luxurious hotel

This totally new concept has been conceived out of frustration and a
desire to develop food that does not conform to the normal paradigms,
where there will be no compromise on quality, ingredients or taste, and
where excellence comes as standard.

Tel: 01246 201 041   Fax: 01246 550 059

Visit our website: www.buckinghams-table.com

give your friend a present

buy taste derbyshire
on line for only £2.95

and we will post it to them FREE of charge*

visit our web site
www.tastederbyshire.co.uk

* UK only

The new Highwayman
Country Pub & Dining

Reinvention...Transformation...Unrecognisable...

The Highwayman in Chesterfield is now open following a total transformation not only of the interior but the whole eating experience!

Signature dishes like our famous 21-day aged steaks can be found alongside the chef's specials which are created daily from fresh ingredients, sourced mainly from British farms.

Here's just a flavour...

Reg Johnson's corn-fed chicken breast

Shepherd's pie made with Welsh lamb shank

21-day aged sirloin steak with traditional garnish

Baked French Brie, mushroom and roasted winter vegetable parcels

Fish of the day – our seafood basket is delivered daily

And that's not all...

Our extensive drinks menu boasts a fantastic selection of wines and house cocktails.

Outstanding food, fresh produce, heaps of hospitality...

The only way to truly experience the new Highwayman is to come and visit for yourself! We look forward to meeting you soon!

Wendy Knott, Restaurant Proprietor

The Highwayman

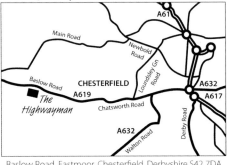

Baslow Road, Eastmoor, Chesterfield, Derbyshire S42 7DA

Call 01246 566330 to book a table

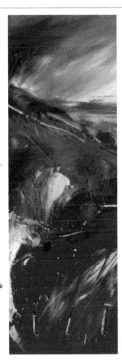
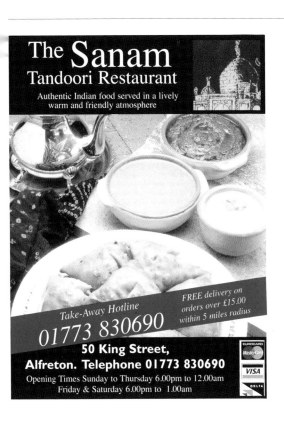

Hotel & Restaurant Guide

Hilton House Hotel
Hilton

Established in 1963, the Hilton House Hotel offers excellent steaks and traditional English food along with en-suite accommodation. They offer a weekly and Sunday Lunch Carvery with a choice of courses, served 12-2pm and 7pm - 9pm weekly and Sunday 12.00-2.30 pm.

The Hilton House Hotel specialises in banqueting, ideally suited for your corporate entertaining, seminars or business meetings and is situated conveniently just off the A38/A50 between Derby, Burton and Uttoxeter, 10 minutes from Toyota.

Beautifully located for your traditional English wedding, with mature gardens and Cedar Tree for your photo shoot, offering formal seating for up to 140 and 180 for evening buffets.

Live cabaret entertainment monthly, the Hilton House has a range of first class amenities, stage, sound and lighting for private hire for parties and cabarets.

The Hilton House Hotel
1 Mill Lane, Hilton, Derbyshire
Tel: 01283 732304
enquiries@hiltonhousehotel.co.uk
www.hiltonhousehotel.co.uk

Limes

Bar & Restaurant Derby

Limes Bar and Restaurant offers an exquisite dining and drinking experience, set on the edge of Derby City's rapidly regenerating centre it's one of the city's newest restaurant bars, and well worth a visit. Located in the Northern Quarter of Derby in Friar Gate, Limes Bar and Restaurant has been extensively furnished and designed with rich chocolate brown tones and dashes of lime green which gives a fantastic modern, contemporary style.

The Upstairs Bar offers a relaxed, warm atmosphere where guests can enjoy drinks and fresh cuisine using the freshest sourced seasonal produce. The menu provides a superb variety of dishes from freshly made soup of the day with rustic bread to such delights as crispy baked cod, noodles, coriander and lime chilli or aromatic duck, plum sauce, dim sum and pancakes with spring onions and cucumber.

There is also a Downstairs Bar which offers a more exclusive, intimate environment, with its own bar, dance floor and ultra chic design, it is the perfect place to hold a private party and is available to hire Sunday to Thursday.

The opening of the new Upstairs Restaurant in the summer of 2007 will provide Limes guests with some of Derby's finest cuisine in a relaxed atmosphere with high quality service.

102 Friar Gate, Derby

For Reservations call 01332 613664
or Fax 01332 299733

Open Sunday - Thursday 12 - 11
(Food Served Between 12 - 9)
Friday and Saturday (Food Served Between 12 - 6)

The Brackendale Restaurant
Knockerdown Farm
Near Carsington Water

Margaret Chamberlain - Proprietor and Head Chef at the Brackendale Restaurant has been in the trade for 15 years. 18 months ago she brought her expertise to the Brackendale Restaurant set in the beautiful Derbyshire Peak near to the popular Carsington Water. The Brackendale offers excellent traditional, home cooked cuisine served in intimate surroundings overlooking the open countryside.

Fully licensed, The Brackendale is an ideal venue for your wedding, convention or party, whether for a buffet or a sit down meal, the Brackendale caters for all, using all local produce and boasts the best homemade Yorkshire Puddings around and succulent steaks on Steak Night Thursdays.

If you fancy a meal set in the heart of the Derbyshire Dales with excellent food and wine then Margaret and her staff will be pleased to see you. The Brackendale Restaurant is well worth a visit!

*Food is served
Wednesday-Saturday 12 noon-2pm,
6pm-9pm
Sunday 12 noon-6pm*

*Booking is advisable.
Children very welcome.*
01629 540880 07891839151

Brocks Café
Ripley
Derbyshire

Brocks café and restaurant in Ripley Derbyshire is situated on the first floor at 5-7 High Street. The head chef is Nigel Brocklebank with 22 years in the Army Catering Corp behind him. Through his hard work and the great team he has behind him they have turned Brocks into a premier eating establishment. On the menu are such delights as their generous breakfast with local fresh eggs, and sausages from the local butcher. Served between 9.30 11.30. But if you miss breakfast don't worry because their lunch time menu, which changes regularly, is again made fresh to order with only the finest ingredients. In the evening Brocks takes on a whole new role - they have introduced a monthly theme night menu which include such delights as homemade pie night, fish night, and Eastern delight night where Nigel produces food to rival the best curry houses in town. Many people have taken advantage of the use of the restaurant for a private function such as for weddings, birthdays and anniversaries, with the well trained and professional waiters and waitresses making your day a special one. Brocks is a great place to go whether you just want to read the paper with a nice cup of coffee or to enjoy a three course meal.

*Brocks Café & Restaurant
5-7 High Street, Ripley, Derbyshire
Tel: 01773 512300*

Horsley Lodge
Smalley Mill Road, Horsley, Derbyshire

Horsley Lodge, which owned and run by Richard and Malcolm Salt. This place continues to impress; serving up a menu of delicious home cooked food fresh as you can get and as local as they can source ingredients.

The ambience is what makes Horsley Lodge's Highlander Restaurant so popular.....it's like a bistro in the country, quality food in an informal contemporary space. Local fresh vegetables, meats, fish and bread are delivered daily

Homemade beef steak pie is still the best seller, and there is always a homemade pudding or crumble to compliment the sweet selection. Even the children's menu is proper healthy food.

You don't need to book at Horsley Lodge....open at 7am for breakfast through to 9pm for dinner, just turn up and the efficient staff with their trendy wireless order pads will seat and serve you pretty smart. Busiest times are 6.30pm in an evening...everyone comes early to ensure a seat, but with over 100 you should only have a short wait. See the full menus at www.horsleylodge.co.uk

The ambience is what makes Horsley Lodge's Highlander Restaurant so popular

The Railway
Cowers Lane
Shottle
Near Belper

There is always a warm welcome at the railway! This great family pub sitting in countryside just outside Belper is fast becoming the venue to be seen at.

Offering a fantastic range of food including specialist Gourmet evenings and the much sought after Sunday Carvery. Under the guidance of Phil and Sue (proprietors) they have made a name for themselves in providing quality food and drink.

The bar menu offers a choice of traditional or contemporary dishes, and the full A la Carte menu includes dishes designed by Phil, using a range of seasonal ingredients. Local produce is used whereever possible.

Children are more than welcome at The Railway, and there are a separate children's menu and a play area outside, close to a decked seating area with heaters for those who wish to dine al fresco.

The Railway hosts a Farmers Market each month. There local produce is sold along with crafts, jewellery and plants.

The Farmers Market is held every 3rd Saturday of the month from 10.00am-2.00pm.
For further information telephone 01773 550271
e-mail: railwayshottle@aol.com
www.therailwayshottle.co.uk

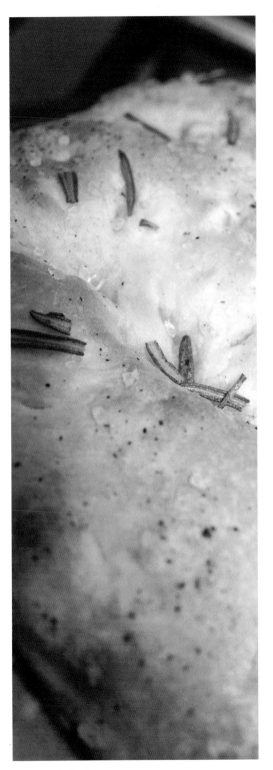

taste derbyshire

would like to thank the following companies for their kind input in supplying the ingredients, equipment and their help in creating the recipes for this book

Chatsworth Farm Shop, Pilsley, Bakewell. 01246 583392
Peak District Dairy, Tideswell, Derbyshire. 01298 871786
M&B Fruits, Derby. 01332 363663
Field House Foods, Duffield. 0141 416 14411
Derbyshire Smokery, Flagg, Derbyshire. 01298 83595
The Honey Pot, Markeaton Park, Derby. 01332 203893
The Original Farmers Market Shop, Bakewell. 01629 815814.

Our thanks also to Denby and Royal Crown Derby for their kind loan of all the dishes etc to present our food on.

Not forgetting of course the photographer Jeanette Howe for her unstinting patience whilst everything was being prepared and cooked.
Contact Jeanette at www.gravityrides.co.uk

Oh, and to Indiana for staying asleep so that her mum could keep cooking!

Above: taste derbyshire chef James Cave with assistant Indiana Burgess